# RACISM AND THE LAW:
# THE LEGACY AND LESSONS OF *PLESSY*

# RACISM AND THE LAW: THE LEGACY AND LESSONS OF *PLESSY*

*Edited by*

GERALD J. POSTEMA

*Philosophy Department, University of North Carolina,
Chapel Hill, North Carolina, U.S.A.*

*Reprinted from Law and Philosophy 16(3), 1997*

KLUWER ACADEMIC PUBLISHERS
DORDRECHT / BOSTON / LONDON

A C.I.P. Catalogue record for this book is available from the Library of Congress.

ISBN 0-7923-4665-3

---

Published by Kluwer Academic Publishers,
P.O. Box, 3300 AA Dordrecht, The Netherlands.

Sold and distributed in the U.S.A. and Canada
by Kluwer Academic Publishers,
101 Philip Drive, Norwell, MA 02061, U.S.A.

In all other countries, sold and distributed
by Kluwer Academic Publishers,
P.O. Box 322, 3300 AH Dordrecht, The Netherlands.

*Printed on acid-free paper*





Printed in the Netherlands.

CONTENTS

GERALD J. POSTEMA

# INTRODUCTION: THE SINS OF SEGREGATION

"The fathers have eaten sour grapes and the children's teeth are set on edge."

Jeremiah 31:29

Just over one hundred years ago, the United States Supreme Court upheld a Louisiana statute mandating segregated railway accommodations.[1] The Louisiana statute, and others like it passed throughout the Southern United States in the 1880's and early 1890's, did not create the structure of social, economic, and political segregation of the races. Jim Crow had already been planted deep in the institutions, practices, and laws of Nineteenth Century American life.[2] Moreover, the "separate but equal" doctrine had emerged in American transportation law through a series of state and federal cases dating already from the 1860's.[3] The legislation of the late 1880's secured this social and legal structure and threatened punishment for anyone who challenged it. Thus, in one respect, in upholding the Louisiana statute, *Plessy* merely made manifest the new form that racism had taken in American life after the demise of slavery. Yet, *Plessy* marks a significant point in American history because it gave new life to the cancer of racism in the U. S. Constitution and the American public mind, undermining the efforts of the Reconstruction Amendments to cut it out. With the separate but equal doctrine, the system of social, economic and political segregation, subordinating an entire race to the will of another and denying members of that race a full and equal place in the civic life of the nation, was publicly

---

[1] *Plessy v Ferguson*, 163 U.S. 537 (1896).

[2] See C. Vann Woodward, *The Strange Career of Jim Crow* (Oxford: Oxford University Press, 1966), Charles A. Lofgren, *The Plessy Case: A Legal Historical Interpretation* (New York: Oxford University Press, 1987), and the many useful references in James Nickel's paper "The Liberty Dimension of Historic and Contemporary Segregation" (this issue).

[3] Lofgren, *The Plessy Case*, chapter 6.

*G. J. Postema (ed.), Racism and the Law: The Legacy and Lessons of Plessy,* 1–24.

reconciled with the demand for "due process" and "equal protection of the laws" that had been written into American fundamental law.

Fifty years of efforts, too often half-hearted and ineffective, to undo the immeasurable damage of fifty years of segregation, sanctioned and protected by the fundamental law of the land, have not removed the bitter taste of racism from American public life. Indeed, the legacy of *Plessy* is rich with bitter irony. The decision is today almost universally condemned as "among the most vilified of all Supreme Court decisions."[4] Yet, as Charles Lofgren amply demonstrates, when the decision was handed down it was "not especially controversial" and largely met with indifference in the nation's press; for all its obscurity and tortured logic, Justice Brown's majority opinion "embodied conventional wisdom" and the case "remain[ed] invisible for a long time after 1896."[5]

Again, now it is widely believed that the decision sought to reconcile segregation with the constitutional guarantee of equal protection by requiring separate facilities to be equal. Yet, as Justice Harlan said bitterly in dissent, "The thin disguise of 'equal accommodations' will not mislead anyone, nor atone for the wrong this day done" (*Plessy*, 562). More ironic, perhaps, is the fact that the majority opinion in *Plessy* never explicitly mentions the separate but equal doctrine,[6] and it is likely that the Court believed the issue of the quality of the accommodations was not constitutionally relevant. It is also ironic that *Brown v. Board of Education,*[7] which allegedly repudiated the *Plessy* doctrine and is widely thought to have invited efforts over the next fifty years to dismantle legislated racial segregation, never explicitly overruled *Plessy*.[8]

A final irony, perhaps, is the fact that now, a century after *Plessy*, American federal and state policies aimed at dismantling the structures of subordination it sanctioned, are themselves being disman-

---

[4] Cass R. Sunstein, *The Partial Constitution* (Cambridge, MA: Harvard University Press), p. 42.

[5] Lofgren, *The Plessy Case*, pp. 5, 196–7.

[6] The term (actually, the words "equal but separate") does appear once in Brown's initial sketch of the challenged Louisiana statute, 163 U.S. 537, at p. 540.

[7] 347 U.S. 483 (1954).

[8] Lofgren, *The Plessy Case*, pp. 204–5. However, Schauer argues that a series of cases after *Brown* so severely weakened *Plessy* that it lost standing as good Constitutional law. See Frederick Schauer, "Generality and Equality" (this issue, pp. 280).

tled systematically, and that the words of Justice Harlan's powerful dissent are used to justify this reversal. Those who find aid and comfort for their attacks on affirmative action programs in Harlan's famous phrase, "Our Constitution is color-blind" (*Plessy*, 559), have reduced to a shallow slogan the compelling moral vision it was meant to convey, a vision rooted in a powerful indictment of the sins of segregation and the cynical devices used to cover the shame and contradictions they cause. As a result, critics have turned a blind eye to its most important lesson.

There are many lessons to be learned from *Plessy*. These lessons, in the first instance at least, may appear unique to American history and constitutionalism. For, surely, the fact of slavery, recognized at the founding of the nation in its fundamental law, and the association of emancipation of African-Americans with the bitter defeat of the Southern States in a bloody civil war, give a distinctive shape to white-black racism in the United States. Yet, racism institutionalized and sanctioned by law and social practice is not unique to the American experience, and the fundamental moral and political principles scorned and cruelly violated by such institutions and practices figure prominently in the political creeds of all democratic peoples. The lessons, in their substance, then, surely have a broader application.

In this Special Issue of *Law & Philosophy*, four philosophers and constitutional scholars take a fresh look at the lessons and legacy of *Plessy.* The essays to follow explore them largely from the perspective of normative political philosophy. This is not the only perspective from which to view the problem of racism and racial segregation, but it is a useful and important one. A number of different themes run through the essays, and each has a distinct focus. Mark Tushnet explores the relation between *Plessy* and other late Nineteenth Century constitutional cases through the lens of libertarian theory. James Nickel traces the devastating impact of racial segregation on basic liberties of citizens. Frederick Schauer argues that the concern at the heart of the moral and constitutional requirement of equality cannot be reduced to a concern about the abuse of categorial thinking in legal and political reasoning. Bernard Boxill explores the prospects and perils of various forms of resistance against racial segregation and discrimination. Uniting these very different projects is a concern to identify the nature of the fundamental moral evil of segregation and the law's complicity in it. In some essays this issue is addressed directly and explicitly, in others it appears more indirectly and by inference. This concern lies at the heart of the opinions in *Plessy* as well. In the remainder of this introductory essay I will highlight this recurring theme. Very different kinds of moral evils are attributed to segregation in these writings. This is not surprising, since an institution as complex, malign, and pervasive as segregation is likely to affect society and its members in a wide variety of ways. The analyses offered, then, are not incompatible. We students of *Plessy's* lessons do well to keep each of them in mind as we attempt to deal with its legacy. Yet, if we are to act responsibly, we need some sense of the relative moral importance of these evils. To this end I add some reflections on the *Plessy* opinions and the essays to follow.

## THE *PLESSY* OPINIONS

*The Majority Opinion (Justice Brown).* Justice Brown never considered whether railway accommodations in Louisiana were of equal quality. This would have been irresponsible, if he had understood the constitutional validity of the Louisiana practice and of Homer Plessy's criminal conviction to depend on the equal quality of the separate accommodations – that is, if he had thought that separate accommodations were constitutional *only if* equal in quality. It is fair to conclude that the relative quality of accommodations was not directly relevant to Homer Plessy's challenge, in the view of Justice Brown. Rather, the central issue concerned whether the Louisiana law mandating separate railway accommodations violated the Fourteenth Amendment's guarantee of equal protection of the law, *even if* they proved to be of equal quality. That is, Brown took Plessy to have put the more fundamental challenge to the segregation statute that segregation *as such* is inconsistent with constitutionally guaranteed equality. Brown answered this challenge by rejecting its implicit interpretation of the scope of the constitutional guarantee.

It is possible to identify two main lines of reasoning by which Brown rejected Plessy's challenge. First, he argued that segregation did not involve constitutionally proscribed inequality, even if the separation was defined and enforced by law. For legal distinctions alone do not entail inequalities, as long as the distinctions serve reasonable goals and are enacted in good faith for the public good. The plausibility of this argument rests, of course, on how "reasonableness" is to be understood. Brown held that it is determined "with reference to established usages, customs, and traditions of the people" (*Plessy,* 550). If "the enforced separation of the two races stamps the colored race with a badge of inferiority" this is due to nothing in the law, but "solely because the colored race chooses to put that construction upon it"(*Plessy,* 551).

Brown's second line of reasoning sought to undermine the challenger's argument that the Louisiana law is constitutionally invalid because it legally sanctioned, supported, and coercively enforced a system of inequality between the races that is pervasive in the society. Brown seemed willing to concede that such *social equality* existed, and by implication to concede that the "badge of inferiority" issued from a deeper and more pervasive source than merely the construction blacks were inclined to put on the law. But, Brown argued, this social inequality in no way threatened the equality guaranteed by the Constitution, since such matters do not (because they *cannot*) fall within the scope of the Constitution's protection. The constitutional guarantee of equality is "absolute" in its sphere, he contended, but its sphere is limited to political and civil rights (*Plessy*, 544). It does not extend to social inequalities, because the law is "powerless to eradicate racial instincts or to abolish distinctions" (*Plessy*, 552). It would be absurd to attribute the aim of eradicating social inequalities to the Amendment, since that is an aim that is beyond the power of any law to achieve. "If one race be inferior to the other socially, the Constitution of the United States cannot put them upon the same plane" (*Plessy,* 552). Hence, social inequalities are consistent with "absolute equality" under the Constitution because the guarantee simply does not and cannot extend to that realm.

*The Dissent (Justice Harlan).* Like Brown, Harlan seemed to assume that the key issue raised by Plessy was not the equality of the accommodations, but the consistency of legally sanctioned segregation with the fundamental aims of the Reconstruction Amendments (*Plessy,* 557). Running through the opinion are concerns about social peace and security and about invasions of personal liberties, but the fundamental evil of segregation, in Harlan's view, lay in its radical violation of equality. Legally sanctioned segregation, in his view, perpetuated in new and subtler forms the system of racial domination and subjection stemming from slavery.

Throughout his opinion, this social and historical context conditioned and shaped his interpretation of every issue. He assumed that racial segregation, discrimination, and prejudice, and the Reconstruction Amendments which sought to undermine them, can only be understood against this background. The Amendments sought to entrench "a positive immunity, or right [of black citizens] . . . to exemption from unfriendly legislation against them distinctively as colored – exemption from legal discriminations, implying inferiority in civil society, lessening the security of their enjoyment of the rights which others enjoy and discriminations which are steps towards reducing them to the condition of a subject race" (*Plessy,* 556). For "in the view of the Constitution, in the eye of the law, there is in this country no superior, dominant, ruling class of citizens. There is no caste here. Our Constitution is color-blind, and neither knows nor tolerates classes among citizens" (*Plessy,* 559). This resounding affirmation of the notion of a color-blind constitution, however, must be understood in its context. This context includes a keen sense of the law's complicity in the maintenance of racial domination, and of the extent to which superficial or formal equalities in the law can mask deeper illegitimate inequalities in which the law is implicated. Against the argument that the Louisiana statute merely "prescribes a rule equally applicable to white and colored alike", Harlan replied, "Everybody knows that the statute in question had its origin in the purpose not so much to exclude white persons from railroad cars occupied by blacks as to exclude colored people from coaches occupied by or assigned to white persons." Its aim was "to compel [black persons] to keep to themselves while travelling in railroad passenger coaches" (*Plessy,* 557). This is a law which, regardless of its formal terms, "puts the brand of servitude and degradation upon a large class of our fellow citizens, our equals before the law" (*Plessy,* 562), for it "proceed[s] on the ground that colored citizens are so inferior and degraded that they cannot be allowed to sit in public coaches occupied by white citizens" (*Plessy*, 560). Harlan concluded, "The arbitrary separation of citizens on the basis of race while they are on a public highway is a badge of servitude wholly inconsistent with the civil freedom and the equality before the law established by the Constitution. It cannot be justified upon any legal grounds" (*Plessy,* 562).

## A LIBERTARIAN INDICTMENT OF *PLESSY*

In American Constitutional theory it is widely believed that *Lochner*[9] and *Plessy* were cut from the same normative and interpretative cloth, both opposing government intrusion in the private affairs of citizens.[10] It is tempting, then, to think that both assumed a basically libertarian normative framework for their constitutional adjudication. Yet, *Plessy's* libertarian credentials appear dubious. The *Plessy* Court upheld the Louisiana segregation law despite the fact that it clearly intruded into the freedom of the railroads and their white and black patrons to bargain regarding nature and cost of the railroad's services. The Court refused to block the efforts of white citizens of Louisiana to alter the contractual relations between the railroads and blacks without paying the market costs for doing so. Moreover, they used bluntly coercive means, criminal prohibition, to do so. If it were acting consistently on libertarian principles, the Court would have decided for Plessy in the segregation case, it would seem.

However, Tushnet suggests that, on closer inspection, the picture from the libertarian perspective may be more complex. One might argue, for example, that the Court in *Plessy* merely allowed Louisiana to assist market forces by effectively signalling the preferences of white patrons to the railroads under conditions that otherwise prevent efficient market signalling. By marshalling a political majority, white citizens provided the public good of segregated railroad cars, accomplishing politically what they could not accomplish in the market due to market-distorting transaction costs. Yet, this argument, in a libertarian assessment, is incomplete at best.[11] Not all public goods are good; not all co-ordination problems are problematic. In some cases,

[9] *Lochner v. New York* 198 U.S. 45 (1905)

[10] See, for example, Sunstein, *The Partial Constitution*, Chapter 2.

[11] On other moral grounds it is entirely unpersuasive, for the apparatus of the law is brought into service of aims and preferences which are objectionable on a variety of moral grounds.

we welcome a swat from "the back of the invisible hand";[12] and one might argue that *Plessy* is surely one such case. For using political power to accomplish the ends of segregation is morally unacceptable, even if it shares certain structural features with legitimate public goods. Libertarian principles clearly recognize the general point of this objection. After all, the value of the market for the libertarian lies in part in the obstacles it puts in the way of collective action.

Without commenting on this argument, Tushnet moves on to consider a second, more complicated argument for the consistency of both *Lochner* and *Plessy* with libertarian principles.[13] In an attempt to reconstruct *Plessy's* argument, Tushnet proposes the following principle, which I will call *the efficacy principle*: government interference in the market is permitted (constitutionally valid) for purposes of protecting public health or safety (which was at issue in *Lochner*) and even to alter the distribution of social power and to approximate social equality (arguably the issue in *Plessy*); but it is permitted *only on the condition* that the laws are efficacious relative to these ends. Tushnet identifies two ways in which the *futility* of laws with goals like these might undermine the constitutional status of these laws: futile *statutes* would simply be constitutionally invalid, whereas futile *common law rules* would lack constitutional immunity against legislative alteration or repeal, even when these laws purport to define contractual liberties. With this principle, Tushnet seeks to make consonant the apparently dissonant decisions of *Lochner* and *Plessy*. Thus, on this analysis, the *Lochner* Court declared maximum hours legislation constitutionally invalid because, *inter alia*, they believed no credible case had been made for the efficacy of the legislation relative to legitimate public health or safety considerations. *Lochner* is seen in this analysis to apply the efficacy condition to the legislation that was under constitutional challenge.

The analysis of *Plessy* is different and more complicated. As we have seen, the Louisiana segregation laws altered the common law rules governing contractual relations between competent parties and so, presumably, interfered with constitutionally protected contractual liberty. If this was not a violation of libertarian constitutional

[12] This is Russell Hardin's phrase. See his *One for All: The Logic of Group Conflict* (Princeton, N.J.: Princeton University Press, 1995), p. 33

[13] Here I isolate what I believe is the central strand of a very complex dialectic. See below, pp. 251–254.

principle, this could only have been due to the fact that the common law rules lack full constitutional protection. They would lack such protection, so the argument goes, if they fail the efficacy condition. In this case, the efficacy constraint is applied not to the challenged legislation, as in *Lochner*, but to the common law rules that are altered by the challenged legislation.

Within this framework, Tushnet considers the following argument. The Court must have assumed that common law rules of contract required common carriers to provide unsegregated accommodations unless market demand called for segregated ones. (Or, more weakly, that ordinary common law of contract authorized common carriers to offer accommodations packages, whether segregated or unsegregated, to the highest bidder.) Moreover, the Court must also have assumed that the aim of such laws was to redistribute social power and achieve social equality. But, as we have seen, the Court argued that racial attitudes are impervious to legal attempts to change them. Thus, these laws are futile. Because they are futile, they are vulnerable to statutory change which would not threaten constitutional liberties. Thus, since the Louisiana segregation statutes only intervene in contractual relations governed by futile laws, they are themselves constitutionally valid. In this way, the apparently disparate results of *Lochner* and *Plessy* reconciled with libertarian principles that, we might suppose, underlie them both.

Clearly, the key device in this attempt to reconcile Justice Brown's argument in *Plessy* with libertarian sentiments is the efficacy principle. But there are good reasons to doubt whether Brown or libertarians would embrace that principle. First, the principle is clearly illiberal in spirit and effect. Its illiberal effect is clear from the application of the principle to the facts in *Plessy.* And while it claims to block legislative invasions of individual liberties to serve broad social goals, it does so *only* when the legislation cannot hope to achieve those goals. It seems only grudgingly to protect individual liberties. Thus, its spirit, too, is hardly libertarian. Moreover, the futility condition, which played an important not to say notorious role in Brown's argument, appears in a form that Justice Brown would hardly recognize. It makes efficacy a condition of the constitutional validity of *statutes* or *common law rules*, whereas Brown clearly regarded it as a constraint on the interpretation of the constitution itself.[14] Finally, Justice Brown would surely reject the reconciliation argument's assumption that the aim of the common law rules of contract was to achieve some measure of social equality. This premise seems entirely unmotivated.

Now, Tushnet does not address these problems. But if his aim was to see how far a libertarian analysis could go towards explaining and justifying *Plessy*, the answer must be that this argument cannot carry that project very far. Tushnet offers no further arguments in pursuit of this exercise, so it appears that we are forced back to our original conclusion that, viewed from the libertarian perspective, *Plessy* was wrongly decided. The Louisiana segregation law is condemned on these libertarian grounds.

Tushnet does not directly address the question of the nature of the (in this case, constitutional) sin of segregation, but an answer is implicit in the analysis he develops. The focus of the argument is on whether or not Louisiana's segregation laws invaded the contractual liberty of the all three parties in the transaction, blacks, whites, and the railroads. If we accept that *Plessy* stands condemned in light of libertarian principles, then its crime was that of permitting the systematic violation of individual liberty by the state, especially liberty to bargain freely for goods and services.

## SEGREGATION AND BASIC LIBERTIES

James Nickel focuses directly on the nature of the evil of segregation. Again, individual liberty is seen to be the victim of Jim Crow, but on Nickel's account, liberty is given a broader liberal characterization. Following Rawls, Nickel thinks of liberty not as a single generic value, but as a set of discrete liberties with regard to a number of activities of fundamental importance to us. Liberties in these areas consist in the absence of limits on one's power, opportunity, or ability to act. This is primarily a negative characterization of liberty, but Nickel's conception of liberty also has a positive dimension, for it entails a claim to protection against invasion, and at least one class of such liberties – rights of political participation – is by nature positive. Moreover, liberty in this liberal conception calls for a system of basic liberties that is *equal* for all citizens.

[14] See above, p. 224.

Jim Crow was a complex, multi-layered structure of exclusions and separations enacted and enforced by law, custom, and attitude. Nickel usefully describes the complex way segregation carved up social space. Complete separation was neither possible nor desirable (blacks provided useful services to whites), but the pattern of separation in shared spaces, and exclusions from key offices and opportunities, expressed and reinforced racist attitudes. Nickel shows that historic segregation seriously infringed a number of the most basic liberties, amongst them freedom of association, freedom of movement and residence, economic liberties, and rights of active political participation. Although, if we view them abstractly, legal and social prohibitions appear to restrict the liberties of both whites and blacks, nevertheless, the system of constraints in fact worked systematically to the greater detriment of the liberties of blacks. According to Nickel, the system of basic liberties under Jim Crow was very unequal. Sometimes this inequality took the form of unequal enforcement of formally equally restrictive laws; in other cases, blacks were explicitly excluded from rights accorded to whites (for example voting rights). Overall, the impediments to action, and the exclusion from offices and opportunities, imposed far greater limitations on blacks than on whites.

This is the basic outline of Nickel's analysis of segregation. But actually his analysis goes deeper, as we can see from his discussion of the special features of *Plessy*. Homer Plessy challenged a part of this system of restrictions, separations, and exclusions. The Louisiana legislation mandating separate railroad cars restricted freedom of association and economic liberties, but not all restrictions of association or economic liberty are morally objectionable. The evil of these laws is made clear, Nickel observes, only when we see them in the context of the larger system of segregation of which they were a part, and in light of their underlying purposes. These purposes, he suggests, were profoundly insulting to blacks. "[T]he message sent by the imposition of a system of segregation and unequal basic liberties . . . was based on the belief that blacks, in contrast to whites, had negative characteristics that made them unworthy of equal basic liberties" (Nickel, p. 274).

Thus, it appears that in Nickel's view, the most fundamental evil of segregation lay not in the restrictions of liberties, or even the manifest inequality of those restrictions, that it enforced, but in the deep insult to blacks and the resulting harm to their self-respect which the system daily and publicly inflicted on them. And, he shows that, although officially enforced Jim Crow has been dismantled, American society still lives with the legacy of segregation in restrictions of economic opportunities, discrimination in housing and employment, and systematically substandard educational facilities.

## GENERALITY, EQUALITY, AND COLOR-BLINDNESS

I argued earlier that the core issue addressed in *Plessy* was not whether the accommodations were of equal quality, albeit separate; nor was the issue whether the Louisiana statute equally infringed liberties of whites and blacks. Rather, it was whether segregation itself was "a badge of inferiority," and hence denied blacks the fundamental equality which was guaranteed them by the Fourteenth Amendment. Frederick Schauer asks the question: Wherein lies the moral inequality of racial segregation? Does it lie, he asks, in the use of categorization as such? Or is there something especially objectionable about the category of race? We can press the question further: If there is something especially objectionable about categorization by race, is it remedied by insuring that the law is "color-blind"? These questions are critical if we are to apply the lessons of *Plessy* to its continuing legacy of racial discrimination.

In moral theory is it customary to maintain that morally objectionable inequalities consist in distributions of goods, opportunities, rights, or privileges on the basis of distinctions that are arbitrary from a moral point of view. In constitutional theory it is tempting to specify further that the wrong of inequality, and in particular the wrong of racial segregation and discrimination, lies in its failure to treat citizens as individuals, in treating them as members of groups rather than in terms of their unique, individual needs and claims. On this view, racial discrimination is seen as a special case of a more general and pervasive evil, that of "non-individualized decision-making". The main burden of Schauer's essay is to show that this is not a plausible account of the injustice involved.

Schauer points out that we often decide on the basis of imperfect generalizations, and sometimes we do so in error, yet in doing so we do no injustice (or other moral wrong). For example, on the basis of reviews in *Consumer Reports* I may pass up a good deal on a Pontiac to buy a Toyota. If the Toyota proves to be a lemon while my neighbor, who took advantage of the Pontiac deal, enjoys ten years of untroubled service, I may regret my mistake. But no injustice or other wrong was done to my local Pontiac dealer. In many cases, non-individualized, "actuarial" decision-making is simply not morally problematic, and certainly not unjust. Similarly, Schauer argues, the wrong does not lie in the use of statistically spurious stereotypes as a basis for differential treatment. For we often find certain stereotypes morally objectionable regardless of their statistical basis.

Schauer concludes that it must be something about the category of race itself, rather than decision by categories, that is morally problematic. But Schauer recognizes that this conclusion raises new questions. Why should racial categories but not others attract moral opprobrium? Can the law avoid such moral opprobrium by carefully avoiding all use of racial categories, that is, through color-blind neutrality? In his essay, Schauer only hints at answers to these questions, and it may prove useful to fill out the argument he suggests.

First, it follows from Schauer's argument that the injustice of racial discrimination lies not in racial categorization regarded *as categorization.* So, blinding the Constitution to this category without paying attention to the special features of the people falling into the categories may not be the solution. These morally distinctive feature of the category of race, Schauer maintains, "lies in the realm of the history of racial generalization . . . " [p. 297] That is, the moral significance of race, and the opprobrium attached to the use of racial categories, is a function of the social, political, and legal history of the use of these categories. The reason why discrimination by race is objectionable, is not merely that racial differences are arbitrary relative to the aims or ends of the law (often, that claim cannot be sustained), but rather that there is a history in America of systematic, institutionalized domination of one portion of the population by another on the basis of race. Schauer does not say any more than this, but it is not hard to fill in the argument. Some of the materials for the argument were supplied by Justice Harlan.

Over the history of its use, the category of race has been primarily a social, rather than natural category. As such, it is inevitably linked to historical relations between the black and white races. The use of racial distinctions in social and legal contexts carries with it to this day the history of oppression of one race by the other. Justice Harlan was keenly aware of this fact and of the complicity of the law in this oppression. A constitution, and strategies of constitutional interpretation, that ignore this history of oppression, and the asymmetry in the relations between the races which results, is "color-blind" but in a fashion that more closely resembles the attitude of Justice Brown than that of Justice Harlan. Racial distinctions are morally and constitutionally objectionable, not because they distinguish between persons on an arbitrary basis, for that is not always unjust, but rather because and whenever they perpetuate and reinforce the legacy of oppression in which the racial categories are embedded. Thus, segregation of accommodations on racial grounds, even where the accommodations are genuinely equal in quality, is a violation of constitutionally mandated equality because it perpetuates and reinforces this legacy of oppression. Where this legacy remains, equality of treatment of citizens under law can never be secured solely by laws that avoid racial categories. Racial categories are not the fundamental problem. The problem lies rather in the social, economic, and political conditions which distort laws that are neutral on their faces to perpetuate that legacy.

## SELF-RESPECT AND THE PERILS OF PROTEST

Like Schauer, Bernard Boxill locates the evil of segregation in the province of equality, but identifies two quite different views of the evil thus construed. These views correspond broadly to the positions taken Booker T. Washington and W. E. B. Du Bois in the debate over black responses to racism and segregation during the *Plessy* era. Thus, Boxill roots his own exploration of the evil of segregation and the modes of resistance to it in the historic debate, especially amongst black Americans, over segregation. Washington tended to see the evil of segregation in terms of the denial of material benefits to blacks, represented by the inequality of public accommodations, and more broadly of economic and educational opportunities. In contrast, Du Bois, like Homer Plessy himself, focused on the offensiveness of the forcible denial of his right to associate with whites in public spaces on terms of equality. Separate railroad accommodations expressed white contempt for blacks and this public contempt was, in Du Bois's words, a "cruel crime". Boxill gives a more precise focus to this charge. He maintains that the harm involved in this crime is a kind of deep psychological injury: it undermines black self-respect. Thus, by a quite different route, Boxill reaches an account of the fundamental evil of segregation which is similar to Nickel's.

Boxill's primary aim is to explore forms of resistance to segregation. He distinguishes three modes of resistance. The first involves the accumulation and subsequent exercise of primarily economic power. This method of material resistance is not essentially public, it was not intended to change the minds or attitudes of the dominant white majority, but rather to wrest concessions from the white establishment and thereby to establish economic equality of blacks. The second strategy, "persuasive protest," is more public; it involves public protest aimed largely at persuading whites of the moral wrong of racial segregation and discrimination and enlisting them in the project of dismantling the structures of domination and inequality. The third mode, involving the exercise of something Boxill calls "moral power," is a special combination of the first two.

In his essay, Boxill explores the nature, efficacy and moral costs of these modes of resistance. The dialectic of his argument is driven by his analysis of segregation as a fundamental threat to self-respect and by the notion, taken from Rousseau, that self-respect of oppressed people is undermined because oppression tends to create a kind of psychological dependence; that the weak tend to live only in the opinion of the strong. Because of this dependency, Boxill argues, the contempt expressed publicly in the systematic and forcible separation of the races (as in the case of the Louisiana legislation challenged in *Plessy*), in the historic conditions of slavery and post-slavery domination, tends to be internalized, and hence threatens to undermine a black person's sense of self-worth.

The method of material resistance was advocated by Washington and the Black Nationalists. In the spirit of Du Bois's critique, Boxill argues that this strategy fails to appreciate fully the depth of the crime of racism and moral dimension of the struggle against it. It fails to acknowledge the offence to the dignity of black persons represented by systematic separation, however equal, and the devastating impact of that offence on the self-respect of black persons. At the same time, Boxill argues, the alternative strategy, protest aimed at persuasion, risks perpetuating rather than ameliorating the effects of inequality on self-respect. This is not only because the efficacy of the strategy is doubtful, but more because, in seeking to persuade oppressing whites to change their attitudes, blacks implicitly accept the view that their existence and sense of themselves depend on the good opinion and approval of whites. Thus, persuasive protest may prove to be deeply corrupting.

Against the backdrop of this dialectic, Boxill identifies two forms of resistance which escape this corrupting effect. First, protest that seeks not to persuade but publicly to challenge the contempt and offence of racism promises to do so. Protest as challenge, as Boxill calls it, consists simply in the public uttering of "a defiant oath of allegiance to morality" which is not aimed at winning the approval of anyone. This form of protest, he maintains, has the beneficial side-effect of bolstering rather than compromising the protester's self-respect. However, Boxill does not rest his case on this arguably rare and rarefied form of protest. Rather, he insists that another, and perhaps the most important form of resistance, involves the exercise of moral power. "Moral power," as Boxill conceives it, is the power of the weaker party in a relationship of domination to impose costs on the stronger party's oppressive actions, costs that are significant enough to force the stronger to take seriously the moral claims of the weaker. The exercise of moral power differs from the exercise of economic power or physical violence not so much in the means it uses as in its aims and intentions. The aim of the exercise of moral power is not just to wring concessions from the stronger, but to bring him to his moral senses, to move him to pay attention to the evidence already available to him that the weaker party has rights which he is violating.

In an extended discussion of Du Bois's example of the resistance of Harris, the slave, against her master, Sevier, Boxill seeks to analyze the mechanism and the effectiveness of the exercise of moral power. Two features of this mechanism are especially clear. First, the exercise of material or physical power works in conjunction with the oppressor's pride and sense of justice. Indeed, the aim of the exercise of this power is, by threatening the oppressor's pride, to awaken his sense of justice, and thus to force him to focus on morally important evidence that he is otherwise able to suppress or ignore. Thus, it is not essential that the oppressed party's power be equal to that of her oppressor; it need only be sufficient to awaken or refocus the oppressor's sense of justice. Second, Boxill seems to argue that, since it is through the exercise of her own power that she forces the oppressor's attention to moral claims she makes in her own name, the weaker party's sense of self-respect supported and enhanced rather than undermined by this form of resistance.

In this way, Boxill argues, the fundamental moral evil of segregation and discrimination is countered. The most devastating moral effect of the denial of status as an equal member of society through domination and subordination is its corrosion of the self-respect of those who are oppressed by it. But there are forms of resistance available which not only can alter material conditions, but do so in a way that reverses the effects of this dependency and restores a core of self-respect.

## THE PUBLIC DENIAL OF FULL AND EQUAL MEMBERSHIP

It appears, then, that the sins of segregation and its modern progeny are many and various. It would be impossible to confine them to a single moral category, even if it were expansively defined. As we have seen, to do justice to its malignity we need at least the concepts of liberty, equality, dignity, and self-respect. Yet, these evils are not all equal; at least they are not equally fundamental to segregation and the problems its legacy poses for us here and now. Indeed, I am inclined to think that we have not yet articulated fully the root of its moral malignity. We can get some idea of this root cause, as I see it, if we reflect critically on some features of the four accounts we have just surveyed.

Consider first the libertarian proposal. Tushnet's libertarian condemns *Plessy* on grounds of sanctioning state intrusion into individual contractual liberty. Since there were three groups of parties potentially involved in the market invaded by Louisiana segregation law (whites, blacks, and the railroads), members of each of these groups were victims of and potential grievants against legally enforced segregation. One need not deny that there is often good reason to regard invasion of contractual liberty as a significant evil to think that, nevertheless, this analysis of the evil of segregation is at best morally unperceptive. There are two reasons for this assessment. First, as it focuses only on legal intrusions into the market, Tushnet's libertarian is silent regarding the evil of segregation itself. For if segregation were to arise from the free contractual acts of consenting adults, libertarians of this sort would have no basis on which to condemn it.[15] The challenge to *Plessy* identified by Tushnet's analysis fails to articulate the ground of our moral revulsion against the system of racial segregation it upheld.[16]

Second, on the analysis suggested, it appears we must conclude that *each* of the parties is a victim. However, the wrong of segregation, first of all and overwhelmingly, is a wrong to blacks; in the light of that wrong, the effects on whites or the railroads lose moral significance. The libertarian perspective, as Tushnet presents it, provides no resources for us to explain this fundamental moral asymmetry. Indeed, to the extent that we can identify an asymmetrical effect of segregation laws in terms offered us by this analysis we are led to identify precisely the wrong asymmetry; for on a fairly standard market analysis of the effects Louisiana's segregation laws, whites stood substantially to benefit from them, and the railroads, not blacks, to suffer most. If we assume with Justice Brown that racial attitudes are "in the nature of things" (*Plessy*, 544), and so are impervious to legal attempts to alter them, and if we assume that whites held the lion's share of economic power in Louisiana, then, if the market had not been distorted by the segregation laws, it is very likely that whites could have and would have bought segregated accommodations from the railroads, albeit perhaps for a modest premium. So, in an unrestricted market, we could expect segregated accommodations to be a common and widely chosen option in public

---

[15] Of course, an enriched libertarian theory that accepts a wider range of individual rights, and authorization of the state to enforce them, might regard segregation, even if it is the product of uncoerced bargaining, as a threat to these rights and in that case worthy of condemnation. For purposes of his libertarian analysis, however, Tushnet assumes a rather thinner background of individual rights.

[16] This is not meant as a criticism of Tushnet's paper, since its aim was not to articulate the ground of our moral objection to segregation, but rather to explore a theoretical position consistent with doctrines at work in late Nineteenth Century constitutional cases like *Lochner* and its legacy. The criticism is directed rather at the theoretical position he set out to explore.

transportation. Of course, where segregation is market-driven, the railroads receive the premium. Thus, while legislation mandating segregated cars does not change the effect of the market process, it does alter the distribution of wealth, for under the mandate, whites rather than the railroads keep the surplus. Thus, on this analysis, while the contractual liberties of blacks, whites and the railroads are equally invaded, actually whites benefit from the intrusion, the railroads suffer most, and the position of the blacks remains essentially unchanged. However, it would surely be a moral mistake to claim that it is the railroads, not blacks, who have the greatest grievance against segregation-sanctioning legislation.

Schauer and Boxill insist that we start our analysis at a different point, namely with the value of equality. Yet, both argue that conceptions of equality that are widely entertained do not adequately articulate our moral objection against segregation, either. Nickel also admits that, as valuable as (equal) basic liberties are, the source of our opposition to segregation goes even deeper. Schauer rightly directs our attention to the historical use of racial categories to structure and legitimate a system of domination. Nickel and Boxill maintain that the moral significance of this history and its effects in the present is best understood in terms of their impact on individual self-respect. This, however, does not give sufficient attention to the public or social dimensions of the crime of segregation. I suspect that only when we fully appreciate these dimensions will we be able to explain why the exercise of moral power – that is, resistance with an essentially public moral dimension – is essential in the struggle against the legacy of segregation.

Let us look first at the public dimension of resistance to racial segregation and oppression. Boxill argues that proper resistance works to change not only the material conditions, but also the moral climate, of social life; for a tense balance of power with the races facing each other with equally potent weapons drawn is not satisfactory for social life. Some substantial measure of moral recognition, mutual acknowledgement of rights and just claims – of equal terms of membership we might say – is essential. Thus, resistance must take the form of protest and at certain points the exercise of moral power; and such resistance is necessarily public. It requires that the oppressor be fully aware of its exercise, for the aim is to force the oppressor to attend to the moral claims of the resisting and protesting oppressed party.

However, if the evil to be resisted is limited to harm to self-respect, then we will not be able to explain why resistance must take this public form. Self-respect supporting resistance need not take a public form. Perhaps the most common and pervasive form of resistance is what we might call "resistance within compliance."[17] James Scott shows that prominent among the "weapons of the weak" are "foot dragging, dissimulation, desertion, false compliance, pilfering, feigned ignorance, slander, arson, . . . passive noncompliance, subtle sabotage, evasion, and deception."[18] When these individual, largely uncoordinated, acts are multiplied many thousand-fold they can impose a heavy cost on structures of domination and can at least take the sharpest edge off the effects of that domination on its victims. However, as Scott points out, "the success [of this form of resistance] is often directly proportional to the [degree of] symbolic conformity with which it is masked . . . Where everyday resistance most strikingly departs from other forms of resistance is in its implicit disavowal of public and symbolic goals."[19] Admittedly, the adjustments and concessions forced by this form of resistance are marginal. The structure of the system of dominance in both its material and its moral or ideological dimensions is left substantially unchallenged. No fundamental material or moral change is likely to be achieved, and none is sought. Why, then, engage in such resistance? we might ask.

The answer is two-fold, I believe. First, while the gains and concessions are marginal when viewed from the perspective of the system as a whole, they may be significant for the survival of individual resisters and their families. Second, it provides an important means of maintaining self-respect and integrity of a sort in a larger social context of pervasive domination that publicly denies individuals recognition as full and equal members. Self-respect, of course, is dependent in part on the affirmation of others, but not necessarily on the affirmation of all, as Boxill himself admits. And, while passive resistance may not fully public, its occurrence and results will

[17] See James C. Scott, *Weapons of the Weak: Everyday Forms of Peasant Resistance* (New Haven, Connecticut: Yale University Press, 1985).
[18] Scott, pp. 29, 31.
[19] Scott, p. 33.

not escape notice of other victims of oppression. Such resistance provides one important avenue of escape from the trap of "living in the opinion of others" (namely, of the oppressors) that so worries Rousseau and Boxill. Scott correctly observes that "[w]hat may be accomplished *within* this symbolic straitjacket is nonetheless something of a testament to human persistence and inventiveness", and, we might add, to the resilience of the human capacity for a sense of self-worth. If oppression threatens to undermine self-respect, human beings often have resources to counter the threat or at least blunt its most devastating realizations.

Nevertheless, we insist that the wrong of oppression (and sin of segregation as an expression and product of such oppression) remains and with it there remain reasons for more public forms of protest. So, there is some reason to doubt that the root of the crime of segregation lies solely in its undermining of self-respect. The wrong, I wish to claim, is denial of a fundamental good to individuals to which they have a claim in justice, which good is not reducible to psychological goods like self-respect, and yet is more fundamental than equal basic liberties or equal material resources (although recognition of this claim arguably should be manifested in the public distribution of such material resources and protection of such a system of liberties). The good is essentially public and social. It is the good of status or standing as a full and equal member of one's society. The corresponding evil is the denial or withholding of this good from those who have a rightful claim to it. This evil is, likewise, public and social. Racial segregation and its malingering legacy of discrimination partakes of this evil.

Segregation was a public and social evil in at least two important respects. First, its cruelties were not attributable solely to this or that individual, its injustice was not the injustice of this or that action. Rather, the cruelties and injustices of racial segregation were systemic, institutional, and embedded in pervasive social practices that gave shape and structure to the lives of whites and blacks alike in almost every aspect and every encounter. Second, this constitutive structure of social relations had both a material and an expressive dimension; the latter are realized in the categories and customs that gave meaning to almost all social encounters. To characterize the latter dimension as "expressive" is not to reduce it to mere subjectivity, to a simple matter of attitudes or opinions. These relations, and the structure they gave to social life, were real and objective. This expressive dimension was objective in the sense that, from the point of view of any individual or group in the society, the terms of encounter and the structures of relations, set the parameters of choice and decision for them. It is probably true, of course, that this dimension was, in some sense, a function of the beliefs and attitudes of members of the society in question, but this in no way blunts the hard edge of its reality as experienced by all members of the society. This structure defines the terms in which members of the different races interact; it also defines who they are as personae in that arena of social interaction. But this must be understood as a social, not a psychological, claim, a claim about one's identity as member or citizen, not a claim about personal identity, or one's sense of oneself. (This is not to deny, of course, that there may be a deep and important connection between them as well.) It is in these terms, I believe, that we can best capture the truth of Du Bois's claim that blacks "will never be real men" until they get social equality.

Segregation, then, was not merely a matter of the private opinions or attitudes of whites in post-Reconstruction America. It was the public expression of a structure of domination, and part of a systematic denial of the standing of blacks as full and equal members of American society. In the historical circumstances of American society after the Civil War, separation of races in public accommodations could carry only one inescapable message: "You, blacks, are not fit to be full and equal members of our, white, society." Separation, of course, was not the only bearer of this message, and it was not necessary in those social circumstances in which other public features, like employment as servants, sufficiently marked the superiority of whites to blacks.[20] This message would have been clear and unmistakable, even if the formal restrictions on the liberties of whites and blacks were exactly parallel and the separate accommodations were equal in quality. For the historical context and the source of the separation measures in political demands of white citizens made the asymmetry manifest, and reinforced the structures of public inferiority and humiliation already in place in the practices

[20] Recall that the Louisiana statute segregating railroad cars allowed black "nurses attending [white] children" to ride in white cars (*Plessy*, 541).

of the society. The "badge of inferiority" was not a matter of "the construction" put upon neutral legal measures by blacks – or whites, for that matter. That is, it was not a matter of how individuals *contrued* the measures; it was a matter of the real social structures and relations which were both publicly expressed and legally enforced by Jim Crow legislation.

In the light of this account of the evil of segregation, it is clear that resistance against this evil must take a public form. The evil was essentially public and social, it could have been resisted effectively only by challenging publicly the structures, practices, and institutions of domination, and their inescapable message of exclusion and inferiority. For this purpose, passive resistance, subtle sabotage, and the other "weapons of the weak" would have been ineffective. The exercise of "moral power," in contrast, commands the use of many of these weapons in a more ambitious, public campaign. Another, sometimes potent weapon is the law itself. While the law is often the bearer and enforcer of the denial of membership, it can also be instrumental in altering that message.[21] It was the thesis of Justice Harlan that the Reconstruction Amendments undertook just such a task.

It is not surprising, then, that Justice Brown and Justice Harlan paid scant attention to the question of whether the separate travelling accommodations were in fact equal in their separate quality; and why Brown sought to deny, and Harlan to assert, the law's complicity in the structure of social inequality. For those were the key issues raised by Homer Plessy's challenge to Louisiana's segregation law. The most important lesson of *Plessy*, as I read it, lies in Justice Harlan's articulation of the fundamental evil of segregation. However, while it is probably correct to say that over the second half of this century *Plessy* has been drained of all constitutional force, American society has not yet fully learned Harlan's lesson. In the *Plessy* era our fathers fed on the sour grapes of racial segregation and a century later our teeth are still set on edge. The underlying

[21] This is the thrust of Cass Sunstein's argument in "On The Expressive Function of Law" *University of Pennsylvania Law Review* **144** (1996): 2021–53, see, for example, pp. 2027–8. I believe that the libertarian scruples, suggested by Tushnet (p. 257), against the use of the coercive dimension of law to alter the message and its underlying social reality are without sufficient moral justification, at least in this context.

evil has proved distressingly resilient, resistant to attempts dismantle its institutional manifestations. We cannot responsibly deny it still exists, but equally we cannot responsibly accept that it is just "in the nature of things". We commit the morally unconscionable error of the *Plessy* majority yet again if we contend that law can and must do nothing to remove its sting.

Netherlands Institute for Advanced Study in
the Humanities and Social Sciences
Meijboomlaan, 2242 PR Wassenaar
The Netherlands;
Philosophy Department
University of North Carolina
Chapel Hill, North Carolina
U.S.A.

MARK TUSHNET

# *PLESSY V. FERGUSON* IN LIBERTARIAN PERSPECTIVE

Decided within a decade of each other, *Plessy v. Ferguson*[1] and *Lochner v. New York*[2] are conventionally understood as intellectual twins. They are taken to illustrate some common failings that today's political liberals believe constitutional adjudication should avoid.[3] And their repudiation is sometimes taken to illustrate beneficial forms of constitutional adjudication. In these comments I hope to question both of these common positions. I argue that *Plessy* and *Lochner* are more different than alike, and that a libertarian perspective often rejected by contemporary liberals helps us understand both why the cases are different and why recent efforts to rehabilitate so-called expressive defenses of liberal legislation may be misguided or at least incomplete in light of *Plessy*.

By *libertarian*, I mean a view of the proper role of government that is limited to provision of the basic conditions of personal security, narrowly defined, and enforcement of contracts voluntarily entered, subject only to narrow exceptions for fraud and coercion, again narrowly defined.[4] *Lochner* indeed can be best understood as a libertarian decision in this sense. It held unconstitutional a state law making certain contracts illegal, in circumstances where, on the Court's analysis, there was neither fraud nor coercion. *Plessy*, in contrast, does not seem at all libertarian, for there the Court upheld a state law making certain contracts illegal even though, once again, there was no reason to think that either fraud or coercion were involved.

[1] 163 U.S. 537 (1896).

[2] 198 U.S. 45 (1905).

[3] I use the term *today's political liberals* to refer to a category familiar in ordinary political conversation, not to one rooted in deep philosophical commitments or analysis.

[4] Government may act, on this version of libertarianism, where otherwise valid contracts have external effects on those not parties to the contract, although a strict libertarian would allow such action only where contractual solutions – between the third parties and the initial parties – were very nearly impossible rather than, for example, merely quite costly to create.

*G. J. Postema (ed.), Racism and the Law: The Legacy and Lessons of Plessy,* 25–38.

Although the membership of the Court did not change dramatically between *Plessy* and *Lochner*,[5] its intellectual orientation apparently did. From the perspective of today's liberalism, both *Plessy* and *Lochner* are anti-liberal decisions, but the latter is libertarian and the former is not.

A libertarian perspective on *Plessy* is illuminating for several reasons. *Plessy*'s repudiation in *Brown v. Board of Education* has come to be taken, on our political and legal culture, to illustrate the essential role of the state in securing racial justice. But *Brown* is in some ways an inapt example for that. It involved one level of government, the national government acting through the Supreme Court, overturing a racial injustice committed by another level of government, the various states with segregated public education system. *Brown* therefore does not really illustrate the value of statism as such, but only the value of one form of statism (centralized, with judicial review) compared to another (decentralized). Seeing *Plessy* through a libertarian lens more clearly shows how the choice between statism and libertarianism might matter than does examining *Brown*.

In addition, libertarianism is not a widely held view in the contemporary legal academy. Invoking it to analyze *Plessy* may show that it has more value than many think. To put it somewhat crudely, we generally want an approach to constitutional interpretation that gets as many right answers as we can get. Libertarianism does better than statism in explaining why *Plessy* was wrong, and neither statism nor libertarianism has much to say about *Brown* directly.[6] This analysis might then open up some space for further consideration of libertarianism as an approach to constitutional interpretation.

Cass Sunstein argues that *Plessy* and *Lochner* rest on the view that the government must be neutral in the face of social and economic relations that exist in some sense outside of or prior to the government.[7] *Lochner* barred legislatures from altering the distri-

[5] Justice Joseph McKenna replaced Stephen Field in 1898, Oliver Wendell Holmes replaced Horace Gray in 1902, and William Day replaced George Shiras in 1903.

[6] Indirectly, libertarianism might suggest that the government ought not be involved in providing education. It would thereby dissolve the problem in *Brown* by condemning all public education, not merely segregated public education.

[7] Cass Sunstein, '*Lochner*'s Legacy', *Columbia Law Review* **87** (1987): 873–919.

bution of economic power between workers and employers. The Court excluded from the legitimate scope of the police power what it called "labor law[s] pure and simple."[8] Labor contracts were freely negotiated, and the purported disparity of power did not mean that employees were coerced into signing any particular contract: If a baker in *Lochner* preferred to work shorter hours than the employer demanded, the baker could move west, become a hod-carrier, or whatever. In light of these real options, the baker was not coerced into signing a contract for long hours. The *Lochner* Court agreed that legislatures could act in response to real problems of public health or safety, which a libertarian would understand as effects of private contracts on third parties, but they could not reject the categories the common law used to determine who had capacity to enter voluntary contracts. The Constitution protected the contracting liberty of those who had the capacity to contract.

*Plessy* too invoked the rhetoric of pre-existing social relations, but unlike *Lochner* it cannot be translated into libertarian terms. Those challenging the statute requiring segregation on Louisiana's trains assumed, the Court said, that "social prejudices can be overcome by legislation." But, the Court continued, "if the two races are ever to meet upon terms of social equality, it must be the result of natural affinities, a mutual appreciation of each other's merits, and a voluntary consent of individuals." The challengers' "fallacy," according to the Court, was "the assumption that the enforced separation of the two races stamps the colored race with a badge of inferiority."[9]

Both cases use the language of voluntary consent, but in significantly different ways. One might put it this way: *Lochner* involved a two-party relationship, between bakers who were willing to work long hours and employers who were willing to pay them for their work.[10] *Plessy*, in contrast, involved a three-party relationship.[11] African-American riders and the railroads contracted for unsegregated service. White riders who desired segregated services could

---

[8] 198 U.S. at 57.

[9] 163 U.S. at 551.

[10] Because the Court found no health or safety problems, there were no third-party effects in *Lochner*.

[11] The following discussion is strongly influenced by Louis Michael Seidman, '*Brown* and *Miranda*', *California Law Review* **80** (1992): 673–753, and conversations over many years with Professor Seidman.

have contracted for them, again in an ordinary two-party contract. Instead they inserted themselves into the railroads' contracts with African-Americans. Nor can the contract for unsegregated services be properly described as having a regulable external effect on whites who were not parties to that contract, for the only such effect is a moral one, the distaste whites feel for allowing others to secure unsegregated services. *Lochner*'s libertarianism defined even third-party health and safety effects narrowly, and certainly could not accommodate third-party moral effects.

As the *Plessy* Court saw things, the challenge to segregation rested on a fallacy about the meaning of segregation. Rather than asserting anything about racial hierarchy, segregation simply was doing what a majority wanted, when not everyone's desires could be satisfied. But *Lochner* suggests another way of satisfying everyone's desires: through a regime of voluntary contract.

The railroads were indifferent as between operating segregated cars and operating unsegregated ones; all they cared about was choosing the system that maximized their profits. If white riders were willing to pay a high enough rate for the benefit of riding on segregated cars, one that exceeded the difference between the cost of operating segregated cars and the cost of operating unsegregated ones,[12] the railroads would operate segregated cars. But if white riders were unwilling to pay the extra costs, the railroads would operate unsegregated cars. The very fact that Louisiana's white railroad riders found it necessary to get the legislature to enact a segregation statute suggests that white riders were unwilling to pay enough, or were unable to aggregate their payments as effectively as they could aggregate their votes.[13] And, of course, African-American riders were perfectly happy to ride on unsegregated cars at the rates the railroads were charging. *Lochner* might suggest that the state law

[12] These costs would include both the direct cost of running a dual set of cars, and the revenue lost from those African-American riders who would have taken an unsegregated train but would not take a segregated one.

[13] Apparently, some railroads in Louisiana were offering segregated services to some riders, although most railroads apparently opposed the segregation statute, in part on the ground that it would deprive them of the flexibility to respond to consumer demand. *Compare* Charles A. Lofgren, *The Plessy Case: A Legal-Historical Interpretation* (New York: Oxford University Press, 1987), p. 17, with Jennifer Roback, 'The Political Economy of Segregation: The Case of Segregated Streetcars', *Journal of Economic History* **46** (1986): 893–917.

barring such a contract violated the liberty of contract of both the railroads and the African-Americans.

Because *Plessy* also involved relations between African-American and white riders, however, the story must be a bit more complicated. The contract the railroads were willing to enter with African-Americans intruded on the interests the white riders sought to advance. Again, however, *Lochner* might suggest the solution: White riders must offer railroads enough to induce the railroads to operate segregated cars. If they do not, we know that however much they care about segregation, they prefer to spend their money on other things. Just as bakery workers could have bargained with their employers, exchanging shorter hours for lower pay, so white riders could have bargained with railroads. If *Lochner* involved a labor law pure and simple because neither side to the transaction lacked common law capacity to contract, so we might say that *Plessy* involved a race law pure and simple, for exactly the same reason.

The legislation upheld in *Plessy* allowed white riders to short-circuit the bargaining process, just as the law invalidated in *Lochner* allowed bakery employees to short-circuit the same process. The Court let white riders use state power to make a contract between two willing parties illegal, instead of requiring them to demonstrate the depth of their concern by voting with their pocketbooks.

A libertarian who applauds *Lochner*, – at least with respect to its refusal to allow legislatures to displace freely bargained agreements – should find it easy to condemn *Plessy*.[14] Indeed, the libertarian aspects of *Lochner* bore fruit a decade later, in *Buchanan v. Warley*.[15] Louisville adopted an ordinance barring home-sellers of one race to sell to home-buyers of another if the house was located on a block with a majority of people of the seller's race. As in *Lochner*, the city invoked the police power, here its power "to promote the public peace by preventing racial conflicts."[16] The Court unanimously struck down the ordinance as a violation of the seller's property rights. The goal of promoting public peace was an important one, the Court wrote, but it could not be "accomplished" by a law denying

---

[14] *See, e.g.*, Richard Epstein, *Forbidden Grounds: The Case Against Employment Discrimination Laws* (Cambridge: Harvard University Press, 1992).

[15] 245 U.S. 60 (1917).

[16] *Id.* at 73.

constitutional rights.[17] The right was, again, the right to sell property on whatever terms the seller and buyer could rely on.

In support of its result, the Court cited *Holden v. Hardy*,[18] a case decided a year after *Plessy* and written by Justice Brown, the author of *Plessy*. In *Holden* the Court *upheld* a maximum hours law for miners, finding that long hours posed a serious threat to the workers' health. A libertarian might reply that as long as workers were aware of the risks, they could bargain for a wage premium to compensate them for the incremental risks of working long hours. In the years after *Lochner*, it became possible to re-interpret *Holden v. Hardy* as a case involving people working in such isolated conditions that they might fairly be treated as lacking common law capacity to contract.

Notably, the Court in *Buchanan* did not take that way out. It did not say, that is, that legislatures could intervene in contracts involving African-Americans because African-Americans lacked common law capacity to contract. That contrasts with the Court's willingness a few years after *Lochner* to uphold a maximum hours law for women only, in part on the ground that women's frailties made the contracts they entered unreliable indicators of the women's true preferences.[19]

A decade after *Lochner*, then, its libertarianism seems to have become rather full-fledged with respect to African-Americans. A decade before *Lochner*, libertarianism did not have as much bite. Had it been deployed in *Plessy*, the result would have been different.

The libertarian argument against *Plessy* rests in large part on the proposition that white riders' revealed preferences in the marketplace, their unwillingness to offer railroads enough to obtain segregated cars and their reliance on state coercion, demonstrate that they wished to interfere with the preferences of railroads and African-American riders without paying the full cost of that interference. More sophisticated modern analyses of legislation, which are compatible with the fundamental libertarian propositions, show why this might not be so.

White railroad riders, the argument goes, faced a coordination problem. Segregation is something like a "public good" offered by a private railroad: If some white rider rich as Croesus could

[17] *Id.* at 81.
[18] 169 U.S. 366 (1897).
[19] Muller v. Oregon, 208 U.S. 412 (1908).

actually offer a railroad enough to buy a segregated railroad car, he would provide the benefits of segregation to all other white riders who preferred segregated cars to unsegregated ones. This rich rider *must* provide the benefit to other white riders: Segregation consists in riding in cars *with others of the same race*, not in riding in a railroad car by yourself. Of course, no individual white rider who preferred segregated cars could actually offer enough. Railroads might prefer to price-discriminate, offering segregated cars to riders willing to pay a premium. But price discrimination is ordinarily quite difficult, because sellers, such as the railroads, find it hard accurately to identify those, and only those, willing to pay the right premium.

Legislation is a way to solve this problem, essentially by substituting a prescriptive regulation for individual contracts when the cost of negotiating such contracts, such as contracts that price-discriminate, is high.[20] To simplify the exposition, suppose (a) that railroads will find it profitable to offer segregated services only if nearly all white riders pay a small premium, and (b) that only whites vote for legislators, who are their faithful representatives.[21] Whites can solve their coordination problem if a majority of them – less than the number needed to compensate the railroads – get together to elect legislators who enact a segregation statute. The statute serves as a signal to railroads that they can profitably offer segregated services: If they do so at a small premium, they will find enough riders.

This understanding of *Plessy* and *Lochner* can be deepened by focusing on the fact that the Court in *Plessy* asserted that legislatures attempting to interfere with the natural social relations of African-Americans and whites were engaging in an exercise in futility. The question is whether law can change the distribution of economic or social power. The *Lochner* Court could imagine that a maximum hours law could indeed change the distribution of economic power, but believed that doing so was outside the proper scope of government authority. It believed that protecting health and safety was within the government's legitimate authority, but held that the law at issue in *Lochner* failed to do so and was therefore unconstitutional.

[20] This is probably the place to note that this is a "problem" only from within a particular libertarian position. From a different perspective, the coordination difficulty is a moral advantage.

[21] This simplification does not change the underlying analysis, within what seems to me a relatively large range of realistic possibilities.

Analogously, the *Plessy* Court may have believed that altering the distribution of social power was within the government's legitimate authority in the abstract, but that all laws attempting to change the distribution of racial power would fail to do so and were therefore unconstitutional.

But, one might think, that was not the issue in *Plessy*. Rather, the issue was whether legislatures should be allowed to displace ordinary rules of contract law, which would allow the railroads to maintain unsegregated cars as long as doing so made business sense (and no longer, if whites were able to offer enough to purchase segregated facilities). What do the ordinary rules of contract law do? They authorize railroads to sell their services to the highest bidder(s): If African-Americans can offer enough for unsegregated services, railroads provide such services, while if whites offer more for segregated services, railroads offer segregation. Now assume that requiring unsegregated services would not change the distribution of social power between whites and African-Americans. That means that whites would offer more for segregated services than African-Americans would for unsegregated ones. Under the ordinary rules of contract law, the railroads capture the surplus the whites have to offer. Under the statute in *Plessy* the whites do not have to make that offer. In this view, then, the issue in *Plessy* was simply whether railroads or white riders would capture the surplus created by white riders' preferences for segregated services.

Here is another version of this argument: The *Plessy* Court must have understood the ordinary rules of contract law to require unsegregated facilities, at least presumptively.[22] But the presumptive goal of unsegregated services could not be reached. Given existing social relations, whites would inevitably purchase segregated facilities, at least if the setting in which they were purchasing tickets allowed them to do so without incurring substantial costs of coordinating their efforts. All that was at stake, therefore, was who would end

[22] In this view, *Plessy* is linked to the Civil Rights Cases, 109 U.S. 3 (1883), which held unconstitutional a federal public accommodations civil rights law on the ground that the common law required public accommodations to provide nondiscriminatory service.

up with the money: whites or railroads.[23] Like *Lochner*, *Plessy* was about the distribution of wealth. But if the Constitution barred legislatures from dictating the distribution of wealth between workers and employers in *Lochner*, it did not bar them from dictating the distribution of wealth between whites and railroads in *Plessy*.

Perhaps the Court believed that the constitutional liberty of contract spoke with particular force to the employer-employee relationship, but had little to say about the relationship between whites and railroads. This might be restated: Perhaps the *Lochner* Court took common law property entitlements to be constitutionally fixed with respect to employer-employee relations, but the *Plessy* Court took the same entitlements to be subject to legislative change with respect to the impact of race relations on transactions between whites and corporations.

A libertarian perspective illuminates this view of *Plessy* and *Lochner* as well. Suppose that efficacy is a condition of legal validity: Legal rules that cannot accomplish their goals ought to be changed, if they are common law rules, and are unconstitutional, if they are statutory rules. *Plessy* deals with the first category: The common law rules cannot reach the goal of unsegregated facilities, so legislatures can, and perhaps should, change them. *Lochner* deals with the second category: The statute, considered as a health and safety measure, cannot promote health and safety, and so is unconstitutional. Having set aside the distributional justification for the maximum hours law, the Court considered its health and safety justifications. It found insufficient evidence that a maximum hours law protected the public's health, because there was no reason to think that bakers working long hours produced particularly unhealthful bread. And it rejected the argument that such a law protected bakers' health, because there was no reason to think that bakers working long hours were at any greater risk than anyone else, unprotected by legislation, working similarly long hours.

One could say much about these arguments on their own terms. For present purposes, however, suppose we accept the view that futile

---

23 The point can be sharpened if we assume that African-American demand for railroad services would not change if railroads instituted segregated cars. Then there is no change in the amount of railroad services provided, and the only question is who captures the surplus. Roughly the same analysis holds if instituting segregated services lowers African-American demand by only a small amount.

legislation is unconstitutional. That view provides another justification for *Lochner*. Consider the argument for the statute the Court found impermissible, that the law was a labor law pure and simple, aimed at altering the distribution of economic power between employers and employees. But the economic case favoring maximum hours laws as a way of altering the distribution of wealth between bakers and their employers is a difficult one to make out. There are circumstances under which such laws will indeed significantly alter the distribution of wealth, but it seems likely that those circumstances rarely occur.[24] The most important set of circumstances arises from the possibility that one incremental change, with few or no distributional effects in itself, will contribute to the development of a political movement that will take larger and more significant steps later: From the maximum hours law in *Lochner* to progressive taxation in the Sixteenth Amendment.

Without taking a definitive stance on that question, however, one can fairly say that a Court willing to find the public health justifications of the maximum hours law in *Lochner* inadequate would probably have found the distributional justification to be an exercise in futility as well.

But *Lochner* may be different from *Plessy* here, in a way that makes the results of the cases consistent. One might think that although a maximum hours law might not change the distribution of wealth as between employers and employees as a class, it might reduce the amount of employment (and incidentally benefit those employees who continue to hold their jobs). Libertarianism as such has nothing to say about the proper level of economic activity, but one can plausibly think that libertarians might believe that, once their fundamental principles are satisfied, policies ought to maximize aggregate social wealth.

---

[24] The best enumeration of such circumstances of which I am aware is Duncan Kennedy, 'Distributive and Paternalist Motives in Contract and Tort Law, With Special Reference to Compulsory Terms and Unequal Bargaining Power,' *Maryland Law Review* **41** (1982): 563–658. I do not mean to assert that minimum wage laws, for example, never have the distributive effects their most ardent advocates hope for, or that such laws always have perverse effects from their advocates' point of view, but only that the direct distributive effects, when they occur, are typically small. The recent controversy over the distributive effects of minimum wage laws does not lead me to reconsider this relatively modest conclusion.

Now suppose that a segregation law simply changes the distribution of wealth between railroads and white riders without affecting the overall level of railroad services provided. If the law in *Plessy* solved a coordination problem it is compatible with libertarian premises, and if it had no effect on aggregate social wealth, it would be consistent with the supplementary principle I have imputed to libertarians as well.

Consider next a different difficulty libertarians might have with the statute in *Plessy.* Suppose that the statute in *Plessy* did solve a market-coordination problem for whites. Recent works on the social meaning of law defend some laws precisely on the ground that they solve such problems, where merely reducing the cost of arriving at agreements would be insufficient.[25] The idea that laws can regulate social meaning can best be understood by contrasting such laws with laws, which we can call *instrumental*, that affect behavior by changing the costs or benefits associated with the behavior. Laws that regulate social meaning are designed to change behavior as well, but indirectly rather than directly. They communicate a view about correct behavior, and thereby induce people to reevaluate their prior calculation of costs and benefits.

The clearest case for a social meaning defense of law is a law barring race discrimination in providing public accommodations, including rail services. Consider a provider who is personally indifferent about whom he or she serves. The provider may believe that he or she would lose business from bigoted customers if the services were provided on an unsegregated basis, and that the loss of business would exceed whatever increment there is from providing such services. A law barring racial discrimination in providing services has two effects on this supplier. The law may demonstrate to the supplier that there is more latent support for, or at least indifference to, unsegregated service than the supplier believed. If so, the law allows the provider to increase his or her business by correcting this misestimate. In addition, the law allows the provider to explain to the bigots that he or she had no choice but to provide the services, and it deprives the bigots of an alternative supplier of segregated services.

[25] *See, e.g.*, Lawrence Lessig, 'The Regulation of Social Meaning', *University of Chicago Law Review* **62** (1995): 943–1045; Cass R. Sunstein, 'On the Expressive Function of Law', *University of Pennsylvania Law Review* **144** (1996): 2021–53.

Suppliers and those customers who desire unsegregated services are better off, but they could not reach this position through voluntary contracts, nor was their problem that arriving at voluntary contracts was too costly.

I believe that the primary motivation for the development of this theme is that scholars have been persuaded that some laws and judicial decisions they find normatively attractive actually have fewer direct beneficial consequences than they first believed. They have been impressed by arguments that *Brown v. Board of Education* had limited immediate impact,[26] and that by the time schools in the deep South began to desegregate, the urban and suburban transformation of the South had proceeded so far that desegregation led to relatively little interracial contact within schools. *Brown* can still be defended, however, on the ground that it made a valuable moral statement, which signaled to African- Americans and whites alike that there might be greater latent support for desegregation than the market or ordinary politics, constrained by a particular history, suggested.

A libertarian would, I think, be suspicious of the uses of law to regulate social meaning. On the most general level, laws regulating social meaning do not secure the basic conditions of personal liberty, nor do they address problems of contractual fraud, coercion, or third-party effects narrowly understood. More specifically, a libertarian would note that mere declarations would often seem sufficient to solve the coordination problems, or to signal greater unexpressed support for one or another position, but laws typically go beyond declarations to include sanctions. And sanctions directed at contracting behavior bother libertarians.[27] In *Plessy*, for example, a libertarian might say, "Let the legislature declare its view – and therefore the view of a majority of whites – that segregation is a good idea, and then see how railroads respond."[28] A sanction might be needed to make credible the railroads' response to African-Americans, that they had no choice about providing segregated services. But that

[26] The most influential work has been Gerald Rosenberg, *The Hollow Hope: Can Courts Bring About Social Change?* (Chicago: University of Chicago Press, 1991).

[27] *See, e.g.* Lessig, *supra* note 25, at 1016 (describing though not endorsing the concern).

[28] Note as well that sanctions bar African-Americans from outbidding whites even if they wanted to.

only exacerbates the libertarian's difficulty: The segregation law blocks people from writing contracts that might be acceptable to all.

A related difficulty is that laws regulating social meaning have no apparent limits. Suppose a declaratory law does not elicit changed behavior. Proponents can respond that the signal the law sent was not strong enough. Sanctions are necessary to make sure that people understand the seriousness of the message being sent, to understand, that is, that there really are others who would like to purchase segregated or desegregated services. If behavior continues unchanged, proponents can repeat their response and escalate the sanctions, up to some unspecified limit set by notions of proportionality.[29] The instrumental benefits of laws regulating social meaning by means of severe sanctions are likely to be too small. Properly speaking, this is a liberal and not a libertarian concern:[30] By hypothesis this sort of law regulating social meaning does not alter the preferences people actually have, but only elicits behavior consistent with those preferences.[31]

Finally, using law to regulate social meaning is inconsistent with the fundamental libertarian assumption that preferences are entirely individual. As Professor Seidman puts it, advocates of segregation did not have a mere "taste" for segregation, but desired "to live within a more general system or culture in which . . . segregation is a part. The ability of individuals to purchase . . . segregated accommodations hardly satisfies those who believe that one system . . . is a moral imperative."[32]

Libertarians reject this view, and therefore have a ground on which to reject the defense of *Plessy* as a form of regulating social meaning. Again to echo Professor Seidman, *Buchanan* is hard to understand except on the ground that it rejects the view that law can regulate social meaning.[33] The Court there treated the transaction as one

---

[29] Lessig, *supra* note 25, at 1043–44, concludes by noting the need to identify limits on the use of law to regulate social meaning, while refraining from proposing them.

[30] Here I use *liberal* in its philosophical sense.

[31] Libertarians do object, distinctively, to laws attempting coercively to change the preferences people actually have.

[32] Seidman, *supra* note 11, at 689.

[33] *Id.* at 698. Professor Seidman uses the term "nonindividualist premises," which seems to me equivalent, at least in this context, to "social meaning."

between a willing seller and a willing buyer, with no external effects. The case for residential segregation on health or safety grounds was surely as weak in *Buchanan* as was the case for a maximum hours law on similar grounds in *Lochner*. But the desire to create a segregated society was patent, and the Court simply refused to entertain it as a permissible legislative goal.

A libertarian perspective illuminates *Plessy* in two ways. First, the connection between libertarianism and *Lochner* suggests that libertarianism might have impeded the development of the American system of apartheid. And yet, to the extent that the statute in *Plessy* really would have been futile, and would only have regulated the distribution of wealth between railroads and white riders, the libertarian perspective in itself does not provide a basis for criticizing *Plessy*.

Second, some recent defenses of socially progressive programs emphasize how they might be instrumentally effective through their regulation of social meaning rather than through the incentives they directly provide. Libertarianism's emphasis on regulating behavior by appeal to reason rather than through coercion, even coercive regulation of social meaning, suggests that the regulation of social meaning through law has an underside. The reason is straight-forward: Someone has to attempt to use law in that way, and whoever does so will have a set of social meanings in place already. They will deploy *their* background and to them uncontested meanings in an effort to change the social meanings of others' behaviors. But, as the law at issue in *Plessy* shows, the meanings already in place – the latent preferences of white riders – need not be defensible. In the end, therefore, the libertarian perspective offered here is at best incomplete. Sophisticated libertarians provide the necessary supplement in their account of individual rights.[34]

Carmack Waterhouse Professor of Constitutional Law
Georgetown University Law Center
600 New Jersey NW,
Washington DC 20001-2075 U.S.A.

[34] As we have seen the typical reliance on background common-law rights will be insufficient as well.

JAMES W. NICKEL

# THE LIBERTY DIMENSION OF HISTORIC AND CONTEMPORARY SEGREGATION

Rereading *Plessy v. Ferguson*[1] invites reflection on historic and ongoing racial segregation in the United States. This essay pursues an enriched understanding of what was – and is – wrong with racial segregation by developing a diagnosis of segregation as an infringement of basic liberties. Justice Harlan's dissent in *Plessy* criticized the requirement of segregation that blacks and whites sit in separate train cars in exactly these terms: "The fundamental objection . . . to the statute is that it interferes with the personal freedom of citizens."[2]

A more standard diagnosis of what was – and is – wrong with segregation is in terms of equality, and uses concepts such as the denial of equal opportunity, economic exploitation, and the imposition of an inferior social and political status. My purpose in focusing on the liberty dimension of segregation is to supplement rather than undermine diagnoses that emphasize the inequality dimension of segregation. But a diagnosis of segregation in terms of liberty has the advantage of avoiding anachronism since it appeals to values that were already widespread in 19th century America. It is also possible that it will grip people who don't find compelling a diagnosis in terms of economic inequality.

We should be careful, however, not to exaggerate the difference between liberty-oriented and equality-oriented critiques of segregation, because the former also appeals to an ideal of equality, namely equality of basic liberties. One criticism of segregation – which seems to be the one that Justice Harlan was making – is that it infringed the liberties of both blacks and whites to associate as they pleased. But another criticism, which partially explains why segre-

[1] 163 U.S. 537 (1896).

[2] 163 U.S. 537 at 557 (1896). A few pages later Harlan said that blacks rightly objected to "the proposition that citizens of the white and black races can be adjudged criminals because they sit, or claim the right to sit, in the same public coach on a public highway" (p. 561).

*G. J. Postema (ed.), Racism and the Law: The Legacy and Lessons of Plessy,* 39–57.

gation wronged blacks far more than whites, is that segregation was a system of deeply unequal liberties.

The first section offers a description and analysis of racial segregation as it existed around the turn of the century in the United States. The second section develops in some detail the diagnosis of segregation as a violation of basic liberties, attending to both its legally and socially enforced components. The final section considers the extent to which the same diagnosis applies to contemporary racial segregation. Throughout I pay attention to what sort of conception of liberty is being employed.

## I. HISTORIC SEGREGATION IN THE UNITED STATES

In the 1870s many whites who had been comfortable with slavery were far from willing to accept blacks as political equals. But political equality for blacks was what the Thirteenth, Fourteenth, and Fifteenth Amendments prescribed.[3] A central part of such equality was that blacks were to be free to use public places and facilities; to move, live, and work where they wanted; and to vote, participate in politics, and serve in public offices. To have blacks enjoying these liberties on equal terms with whites was unacceptable to many southern whites[4], and as soon as they were sure they could get away with it they constructed a system – segregation, or "Jim Crow" – that reimposed political inequality by depriving blacks of the vote and by restricting important liberties such as freedom of association, freedom of movement, and free choice of occupation.[5] By the 1890s,

[3] For a history of "Freedom and Repression in the Post-War South." see Paul Finkleman, "Introduction: The Law of Freedom," *Chicago-Kent Law Review* **70** (1994): 325–368. See also David A. J. Richards, *Conscience and the Constitution: History, Theory, and Law of the Reconstruction Amendments* (Princeton, N.J.: Princeton University Press, 1993).

[4] This was true of many northern whites as well. Segregation of free blacks in northern cities was common in the early nineteenth century, and hence northern segregation antedated the southern version. See Leon F. Litwack, "Segregation in the Antebellum North," in Joel Williamson, ed., *The Origins of Segregation* (Boston: D. C. Heath, 1968), pp. 88–95.

[5] See C. Vann Woodward, *The Strange Career of Jim Crow* (Oxford: Oxford University Press, 1966); John Hope Franklin, *From Slavery to Freedom: A History of Negro Americans* (New York: Alfred A. Knopf, third edition, 1967); and Joel Williamson, *After Slavery* (Chapel Hill: University of North Carolina Press, 1965).

when Plessy's unsuccessful challenge to segregated trains was made, many areas of life had been formally divided into different areas for blacks and whites.

Segregation involved both *exclusion* and *separation*. Exclusion of blacks occurred in areas such as voting, political participation, and service in public offices. Substantial numbers of blacks voted during Reconstruction and shortly thereafter. But efforts by the Ku Klux Klan and others to discourage blacks from voting began early on, and by the late 1870s a widespread effort to disfranchise blacks was underway. Means of doing this included complicated registration and voting procedures, poll taxes, literacy tests, and white primaries.[6]

Segregation applied to most areas of life. Areas of separation included churches, schools, neighborhoods, the workplace (although segregation here was limited by the important economic role of black farmers and workers), and public facilities such as trains and busses, hospitals, stores, restaurants, hotels, parks, and beaches.[7] The main places where blacks and whites mixed together were on the streets and roads, in (some) stores, and in (some parts of) the workplace.

To analyze segregation in more detail, we can say that it divided social space into four sectors. First, there were *shared and unsegregated sectors* such as roads and sidewalks. Second, there were *shared but segregated sectors* such as trains and (some) parks. Here the same (or an inferior version of the same) services or facilities were available to blacks as to whites, but there were segregated areas within them. This type of social space was the natural home of the separate but equal doctrine that *Plessy v. Ferguson* sanctified. Third, there were *unshared and segregated areas* such as schools, churches, and potential marriage partners. This area offered blacks indepen-

[6] See Franklin, *From Slavery to Freedom*, pp. 324–343, for a good account of disfranchisement.

[7] Franklin gives a nice summary of this:

> Beginning in Tennessee in 1870, Southerners enacted laws against intermarriage of the races in every Southern state. Five years later, Tennessee adopted the first "Jim Crow" law and the rest of the South rapidly fell in line. Negroes and whites were separated on trains, in depots, and on wharves. Toward the end of the century the Negro was banned from white hotels, barber shops, restaurants, and theaters, after the Supreme Court in 1883 outlawed the Civil Rights Acts of 1875. By 1885 most Southern states had laws requiring separate schools.

*From Slavery to Freedom*, p. 342.

dence from whites and the opportunity to develop and run their own institutions. But it also limited blacks to what was available in their own community. And fourth, as we saw earlier, there were areas of *exclusion* such as voting and other forms of political participation. Movie theaters, for example, could fall into any of these sectors depending on how they were arranged. They could be shared and unsegregated if blacks and whites were free to attend the same theaters and could sit wherever they wanted (the arrangement we have today). They could be shared and segregated if blacks and whites used the same movie theater but blacks were restricted to a particular section such as the balcony (the most common arrangement during segregation). Theaters could be unshared and segregated if there were completely separate ones for blacks and whites. Or there could be exclusion if there were no movie theaters that blacks were permitted to attend.

The means whereby segregation was imposed varied by sector. Segregation in areas of government provision or facilitation such as elections, police and legal services, schools, parks, and public transportation was explicitly decreed and enforced by law. Segregation in stores, restaurants, and theaters was sometimes decreed by law, but was also sometimes structured and enforced by the whites who owned and operated the facilities – with backup support from the police if needed. For example, eating establishments usually refused to serve blacks at tables or counters, but were sometimes willing to sell food for consumption outside. Social segregation was often imposed through custom and social pressure – with facilitation from the system of segregated schools and churches, and with backup support from vigilantes and lynch mobs.

In the economic area, segregation and exclusion were often restrained by the economic value of blacks as workers and customers. For example, whites often wished to employ black sharecroppers and laborers, and hence had reasons to tolerate the racial togetherness this required. Initially, sharecropping, manual labor, and domestic service were the main economic options available to blacks. Later, as educational opportunities improved, some African-Americans found jobs as teachers in black schools, as shopkeepers in black neighborhoods, and as doctors for black patients. But segregation served to keep blacks mostly located in certain occupations and parts of the economy. It did this through the limitation of educational opportunities and discrimination in hiring. Blacks were systematically excluded from positions having authority over whites.

## II. SEGREGATION AS A VIOLATION OF BASIC LIBERTIES

The Civil Rights Movement of the 1960s made extensive use of the rhetoric of freedom. Was this just an attempt to play to favored American values, or were there important ways in which segregation deprived people of liberty? The rhetoric of liberty rightly played an important role in emancipation, when the slaves were literally set free from slavery, but perhaps the 20th century use of this rhetoric is just a carryover from the past that now has little substance.[8] In this section I attempt to show that this is not true; that historic segregation involved substantial violations of basic liberties.[9]

Keeping apart two groups that live in the same territory and under the same government usually requires the use of social and legal norms that tell people quite clearly where they can and can't live, where they can and can't go to school, where they can and can't work, and with whom they can and can't associate. This is particularly true if one of the groups doesn't want to be segregated, or so thoroughly segregated. Segregation's standing barriers to action in key areas of liberty were often reinforced through dramatic events such as arrests, beatings, murders, and lynchings, and hence deprivations of liberty had a saliency that structural inequalities often lacked. Because of this, it is not surprising that a familiar complaint against segregation was that it made African-Americans unfree.

### *A. A Negative Conception of Liberty*

The claim that historic segregation violated basic liberties will be most robust and have the widest appeal if it does not depend on an

---

[8] See Robert William Fogel, *Without Consent or Contract: The Rise and Fall of American Slavery* (New York: W. W. Norton, 1989), pp. 393–400 for a concise account of what was wrong with slavery. The first point in his moral indictment is that "slavery permitted one group of people to exercise unrestrained personal domination over another group of people" (p. 394).

[9] For legal and historical essays exploring this theme, see the symposium on "The Law of Freedom" in the *Chicago-Kent Law Review* **70** (1994): 325–800.

exotic or contentious conception of liberty. Accordingly, the conception of liberty that I will use in discussing segregation will be standard and largely "negative."[10] It takes liberties to consist in the absence of impediments to action in specific areas. The areas of liberty that I will focus on are ones that are widely recognized as important or "basic."[11] Unfreedom in some area, on this view, is having one's choice and action in that area blocked by external barriers such as social or legal prohibitions, discrimination, and threats of harm or violence.[12] On this view of freedom, not having enough money to buy a trip to China is not a source of unfreedom, but being unable to buy such a trip because travel to China is legally forbidden or because one is black and travel agents refuse to sell tickets to blacks *is* a restriction of one's freedom. On the negative view, freedom is concerned with some but not all of the things that limit a person's power, opportunities, and actual abilities to act in certain ways.

There are, however, some "positive" elements in the conception of liberty that I will use. One is a claim against government to protect one's basic liberties. Another element that might be considered "positive" is found in the fact that I will take freedom of politi-

---

[10] On the contrast between negative and positive conceptions of liberty see Isaiah Berlin, *Two Concepts of Liberty* (Oxford: Oxford University Press, 1958); and Gerald MacCallum, "Negative and Positive Freedom," *Philosophical Review* **76** (1965): 312–334.

[11] John Rawls takes respect for basic liberties to be the first requirement of social justice. See John Rawls, *A Theory of Justice* (Cambridge, Mass.: Harvard University Press, 1971), and *Political Liberalism* (New York: Columbia University Press, 1993). See also James W. Nickel, "Rethinking Rawls's Theory of Liberty and Rights," *Chicago-Kent Law Review* **69** (1994): 763–785.

[12] In analyzing the liberty dimensions of historic and contemporary racial segregation I will focus on legal and social barriers to action and choice that are external and imposed by others. An alternative approach might emphasize internal barriers to action such as hopelessness, an inability to imagine feasible alternative actions and ways of living, dependency on welfare with a consequent lack of confidence in one's ability to cope with the world of work, and aversion to facing possible discrimination and rejection. One might argue that many inner-city blacks suffer from these sorts of internal barriers to action as a result of racism, segregation, and discrimination, and that the unfreedom of many black Americans and its connection with segregation cannot be understood or combatted without taking these sorts of internal barriers into account. For a discussion of this sort of conception of liberty, see Nancy J. Hirschman, "Toward a Feminist Theory of Freedom," *Political Theory* **24** (1996): 46–67.

cal participation to imply a duty of governments to offer citizens opportunities to vote in regular and meaningful elections.

It might be objected here that to give an adequate analysis of historic and contemporary segregation we need a stronger, more positive conception of liberty that equates unfreedom with powerlessness. When riots and violent confrontations with police occur in largely-black urban areas, as they recently did (November 1996) in St. Petersburg, Florida, community leaders who attempt to diagnose the causes of the violence often report that many black residents feel powerless. They feel trapped in a bad situation and unable to do much to escape it. Perhaps they are not literally powerless in the sense of being unable to do anything, but their effective abilities to act in important areas such as education, housing, and business are substantially lower than those of most whites. And these lower-than-average abilities to act are at least partially due to historic segregation and ongoing discrimination. Here one might follow Amartya Sen in defining equal freedom as equal functionings and capabilities.[13] But I will not take this approach for two reasons. One is that, as noted above, my argument will be of more general interest if it doesn't depend on a strong and controversial conception of freedom. The other is that this conception of freedom collapses the distinction between two valuable ideals: equality of basic liberties and equality of opportunity. I endorse both of these ideals, and will illustrate below some of the ways that they are linked, but I think that they are interestingly different and are better left separate so that they can make their distinctive contributions.

### *B. Unequal Liberties*

As I suggested in the introduction, a society could be criticized on liberty grounds if no one enjoys basic liberties, or if some people enjoy them while others don't. The latter criticism appeals to an ideal of *equal* basic liberties. My treatment of historic segregation will make both kinds of criticisms. It will say that segregation made everyone – that is, both blacks *and whites* – less free in important areas such as association. It will also criticize segregation for being a system of unequal liberties, for giving whites freedom in areas

[13] Amartya Sen, "Freedom Of Choice: Concept and Content," *European Economic Review* **32** (1988): 269–294.

where blacks were restrained. A liberty to do something is unequal if one group is free to do that thing and another isn't, or if one group has a much larger liberty in that area than the other.

Most people today who espouse liberty as a political ideal are in favor of equal basic liberties, i.e. liberties that all citizens enjoy in roughly the same measure or degree. But this was not true in 19th century America. Many whites valued liberty, but were not in favor of giving it fully to blacks. They favored, and ultimately imposed, a system of unequal freedom.

Real liberty is a matter of the genuine absence of certain barriers, not merely of laws saying that those barriers should be absent. And two persons or groups enjoy equal liberty when they both enjoy the actual absence of certain impediments to action, not merely the same prescriptions of liberty. Partisans of liberty promote legal prescriptions of liberty as a means to real liberty, but as with other means these legal prescriptions sometimes get confused with their end. So if the law proclaims equal liberty for whites and blacks, but only whites enjoy the freedom and have it protected by government, this is still unequal liberty. And if the law prohibits sexual relations between blacks and whites, but punishes blacks but rarely whites when interracial liaisons occur, this is also unequal liberty (or if you prefer, unequal *un*freedom).

### *C. Segregation generally*

If we look at segregation as a whole, it substantially infringed freedom of association; freedom of movement and residence; free choice of occupation and other economic liberties; and liberties to vote and participate politically. It also created a scheme of unequal liberties in most of these areas. Although these liberties all receive constitutional recognition in the United States today, my arguments are not intended as arguments in constitutional law. They are rather arguments in political philosophy, or in the theory of human rights.[14]

---

[14] All of the basic liberties discussed here are declared to be universal human rights in contemporary human rights documents. For example, the *International Covenant on Civil and Political Rights* (1966) treats freedom of association in article 22; freedom of movement and residence in article 12; free choice of occupation in article 8; and liberties to vote and participate politically in article 25. For an attempt to develop a philosophy of human rights, see James W. Nickel, *Making Sense of Human Rights* (Berkeley: University of California Press, 1987).

*1. Freedom of association*

Association with others takes many forms including friendship, love and sexual intimacy, family ties, the relations of neighbors and fellow citizens, religious affiliations, and all sorts of social, political, and commercial alliances.[15] People's interest in freedom of association is the interest in not having substantial barriers to entering, refraining from entering, and withdrawing from such relations.

Historic segregation severely limited the freedom of blacks and whites to associate across racial lines. It placed substantial social and legal barriers in the way of those who would form interracial friendships, love affairs, families, churches, schools, or community organizations. To prevent the formation of such relations it kept blacks and whites apart, putting them in separate neighborhoods, schools, churches, and occupational areas. When such associations formed in spite of these measures, they were subject to legal prohibition, as with interracial marriages, and to severe social sanctions including violence.

Keeping blacks from associating with whites was a key purpose of segregation. But segregation also limited the liberty of whites to associate with blacks. Most whites didn't want to associate with blacks, except perhaps on a business basis in some areas, but the relevance of this to liberties is small for two reasons. First, large populations are seldom uniform in their desires. Some whites did want to associate with African-Americans for purposes such as friendship, family relations,[16] religious evangelism, economic profit, and sexual relations. Second, liberties can be valuable even though only a few people desire to make use of them. For example, the liberty to leave one's historic place and take up residence elsewhere is valuable even when most people prefer to and actually do stay

---

[15] On freedom of association see Kenneth Karst, "Paths to Belonging: The Constitution and Cultural Identity," *North Carolina Law Review* **64** (1986): 303–377; and Aviam Soifer, " 'Toward a Generalized Notion of the Right to Form or Join an Association': An Essay for Tom Emerson," *Case Western Reserve Law Review* **38** (1988): 641–670.

[16] Recall *Loving v. Virginia*. 388 U.S. 1 (1967) (ruling unconstitutional Virginia's prohibition of interracial marriage). See also the account of interracial marriages in Mississippi in 1870–85 in Vernon Lane Wharton, "Jim Crow Laws and Miscegenation," in Joel Williamson, ed., *The Origins of Segregation* (Boston: D.C. Heath, 1968): 14–20, at p. 19.

put. In my opinion, segregation significantly infringed the freedom of association of both blacks and whites.

But segregation also created a system of unequal liberties in the area of association. Whites were far less likely to be punished, legally or socially, for associating with blacks than blacks were for associating with whites.

The denial of associative liberties had real costs to blacks because whites controlled most of the assets they needed in order to make educational and economic progress. By being blocked from free access to whites, blacks were thereby blocked from access to many of the assets that whites controlled. Thus, unequal liberties contributed greatly to unequal opportunities.

A possible objection to the analysis presented here is that a condemnation of segregation in terms of freedom of association doesn't take seriously enough the liberty to dissociate – which is surely an important part of freedom of association.[17] What about the liberty interests of those whites who didn't want to associate with blacks, and who didn't want their children to have opportunities to associate with blacks? It is clear that freedom of association leaves one free to refuse to be friends with, talk to, or remain located close to persons one finds distasteful for whatever reason. But it is an entirely different matter when one group uses the power of law and threats of social violence to keep another entire group away from it and its children. Freedom of association doesn't give a dominant group the right to confine an entire group in a separate social realm.

*2. Freedom of movement*

A person who is imprisoned or even under house arrest suffers greatly reduced abilities to act in a multitude of areas. Freedom of movement is the liberty to go – and stop – where one pleases within the limits of respect for the liberty and rights of others. The American system of apartheid, unlike the South African one, did not use internal passports and roadside checkpoints to monitor whether blacks were in, or traveling to, areas for which they had residence

[17] On dissociation see Pamela J. Smith, "We are Not Sisters: African-American Women and the Freedom to Associate and Dissociate," *Tulane Law Review* **66** (1992): 1467–1515; and Robert W. McGee, "The Right to Not Associate: The Case for an Absolute Freedom of Negative Association," *UWLA Law Review* **23** (1992): 123–148.

permits. Segregation in the U.S. nevertheless substantially infringed freedom of movement because it prevented blacks from going – and stopping – where they pleased without fear of harassment, violence, or arrest. Segregation was a system of unequal liberties of movement. Blacks were expected to stay out of white areas unless they had white-authorized business in them, and some white towns forbade blacks to stay after sundown.

Further, the Jim Crow system inhibited the ability of blacks to travel by excluding them from the only available hotels and restaurants along public railroads and highways. Plessy presents us with a skewed picture of historic segregation since blacks were on the same train, albeit in separate cars. As long as blacks were on the same trains, they had the same opportunities for travel as whites – assuming they could afford the tickets. But in many areas there were completely separate systems of services, and the fact that blacks were almost always poorer and in some areas fewer than whites meant that the services available to them were sometimes very limited. Hotels, for example, didn't usually have separate areas within the same hotel for whites and blacks. The social space for hotels was not shared and segregated, as with trains, but was rather unshared and segregated. In cities with lots of blacks there were rooming houses and hotels for blacks, but along highways and in cities with few blacks, places to stay were often severely limited. In general, if people are restricted to the services and opportunities offered by their own communities, smaller and poorer groups will often face severely restricted options. This is one of the many links between the denial of basic liberties and the denial of equal opportunity.

*3. Free choice of residence*

Residence is closely related to movement; it is the liberty to choose a new place as one's temporary or permanent home, along with the liberty to resolutely stay in one's native place if one wishes. As we just saw, during segregation blacks were unwelcome in many areas, especially if they showed any inclination to stay. African-Americans were expected to reside in their own neighborhoods, and if they moved it had to be from one black area to another. Discrimination in access to housing was – and continues to be – a major barrier to free choice of residence by blacks. Eventually, many blacks did succeed in moving to the north, midwest, and west. But when they arrived housing discrimination usually restricted them to particular areas of town.

Segregation didn't much limit the liberty of whites to enter and stop in black areas, or to reside where they wished. The restrictions imposed on blacks' freedoms of movement and residence created a scheme of unequal liberties.

*4. Free choice of occupation and other economic liberties*

My main concern here is the freedom to choose and pursue an occupation, employment, or business. Related liberties include the freedom to hold and transfer property on equal terms with other citizens, and the freedom to pursue and enter into economic arrangements and enterprises on equal terms with other citizens. Under slavery occupational choice for blacks was almost totally absent. Slaves did whatever sort of labor was ordered by their masters, and they couldn't leave their jobs or try to find new ones. Emancipation gave blacks the liberty to choose their jobs or line of work, but their options were greatly limited by poverty, lack of education, and the fact that only a few areas of work were open to them. Initially, blacks were restricted to sharecropping, manual labor, and domestic service. Later, with industrialization, blacks had access to jobs in steel mills and factories, but were frequently restricted to certain job categories. As with discrimination in housing, job discrimination followed blacks as they moved north and west. Segregation violated free choice of occupation because it confined blacks to certain sorts of jobs through discrimination in education and hiring. It also restricted economic opportunities by limiting where blacks could go and stay, and by limiting associational opportunities that could lead to employment or business. Segregation limited the economic liberties of whites since it prevented them from employing blacks in occupational areas that were reserved for whites – and sometimes these restrictions had significant economic costs. But the main criticism here is in terms of unequal liberties. Segregation severely restricted free choice of occupation for blacks, while imposing no such restrictions on whites.

In this section and the previous one, I have assumed that people can be made unfree by discrimination. But is this plausible? If blacks are legally free to seek any job, for example, but are subject to job discrimination from a significant percentage of employers, does this infringe their liberty to free choice of occupation? I think the answer is affirmative. When the members of a group face discrimination in hiring today, they typically don't face a uniform or monolithic policy. Some employers will evaluate their qualifications fairly and not discriminate; others will discriminate a little in the sense that they hold people from the group to a stricter standard of qualification; yet others will discriminate a lot but might be willing to hire people from the group in exceptional cases; and still others may be unwilling to hire people from the group under any circumstances. Because of this, discrimination isn't always an insuperable barrier to getting a job. Sometimes one can get around it by being very qualified, or by having the right connections, or through ingenuity. However, discrimination is still an impediment to liberty. But don't barriers have to be insuperable to be impediments to liberty? I don't think so. A legal prohibition of doing something backed by a substantial fine or penalty if one is caught and convicted is a paradigm of a barrier to liberty. Yet legal prohibitions are usually far from insuperable barriers to doing what is prohibited.

*5. Political liberties*

These include freedoms to vote in fair and meaningful elections, to petition government, to serve in public office, to engage in political speech, protest, organization, and assembly, and to register complaints of violations of law and use state and federal courts.[18] In most Southern states African-Americans were excluded from voting and other forms of political participation from roughly 1890 to 1965. Disfranchisement of blacks allowed whites to avoid living under the "rule" of blacks, and helped stabilize the Jim Crow system by preventing blacks from using their votes to protest segregation and inequality. Other rights of political participation were violated as well. In the South it was very dangerous for blacks to make political speeches, to assemble and protest, and to organize politically.[19]

Political liberties are the clearest example of how segregation created a system of unequal liberties. After 1990, whites had a monopoly

---

[18] See Christopher Waldrep, "Black Access to Law in Reconstruction: The Case of Warren County, Mississippi," *Chicago-Kent Law Review* **70** (1994): 583–624.

[19] See *NAACP v. Alabama ex rel. Patterson*, 357 U.S. 449 (1958) (rejecting as unconstitutional Alabama's demand for the membership lists of the state chapter of the NAACP).

on political power, and blacks had extremely limited political liberties. To use the analysis of social space presented in the first section, political activity was not even a shared but segregated area with different systems of political participation for blacks and whites.[20] Until the final decades of southern segregation, political activity was simply an area from which blacks were excluded.

### *D. Plessy v. Ferguson*

Plessy's challenge was to just one small part of the Jim Crow system. He said that he shouldn't be subject to criminal penalties for refusing to sit in the black section of the train. The Louisiana statute requiring segregation on trains imposed a fine or imprisonment for sitting in the wrong section. It also penalized railway officials if they failed to administer the racial division. It is clear that this statute limited liberties; it used criminal penalties to require blacks and whites to sit in designated cars and to prohibit them from sitting together. But were the liberties sufficiently important ones, and was the restriction of those liberties sufficiently large?

It is clear that important liberties were restricted by segregation on trains. Freedom of association was limited by a scheme that required blacks and whites to stay apart while traveling on trains. Freedom of movement was limited by the fact that blacks who wished to travel by train had to submit to a humiliating system of segregated cars. And important economic liberties were limited by the fact that blacks could not work with, work for, or sell things to whites on trains because they could not enter the cars reserved for whites.

It might be argued, however, that the restrictions that train segregation imposed on these liberties were not very large, and hence that train segregation by itself can't be viewed as a significant infringement of basic liberties. Suppose that for safety reasons train passengers were required to sit in single-person "capsules" that would protect them in case of a train crash. This requirement would greatly restrict associational and economic opportunities on trains, but people would still have ample opportunities for association elsewhere, and thus we would probably conclude that this safety

---

[20] The South African system of apartheid used shared but segregated systems of political participation by having a separate legislative branch for "coloreds."

requirement does not restrict associational opportunities to a significant degree.

One answer to this objection is that in evaluating small restrictions on liberty we should attend to their purposes. The purpose of a small restriction on liberty is relevant not only to seeing if there is a justification for the restriction, but also to understanding its meaning. A restriction on association intended to promote train safety may be less objectionable on liberty grounds than a restriction on association intended to restrict association between two groups. One of the main purposes of segregation was to restrict association between blacks and whites, and it did this in a multitude of areas.[21] Segregation kept blacks separate for whites in most spheres of life, and the beliefs of whites about blacks that made them demand such separation were profoundly insulting to blacks.[22] Another response is that blacks didn't have ample opportunities elsewhere for association with whites. Segregation greatly reduced associational opportunities between blacks and whites. It initiated the still ongoing social isolation of blacks.

*E. An objection*

Does the liberty diagnosis of segregation give an adequate explanation of how Jim Crow was mainly an injustice to blacks? An adequate diagnosis of what was wrong with segregation needs to explain its asymmetrical character: how it deeply wronged African-Americans while hurting whites to a much smaller degree. Yet under a liberty-oriented diagnosis, we see that many of the barriers imposed by segregation limited the liberties of both blacks *and whites*. Hence it seems doubtful that a liberty-oriented diagnosis of what was wrong with segregation yields an adequate account of the

---

[21] For a good discussion of the purposes that segregation served for both blacks and whites, see Joel Williamson, *After Slavery*, pp. 275–279.

[22] One of the most outrageous passages in the majority opinion in *Plessy* denies this:

> We consider the underlying fallacy of the plaintiff's argument to consist in the assumption that the enforced separation of the two races stamps the colored race with a badge of inferiority. If this be so, it is not by reason of anything found in the act, but solely because the colored race chooses to put that construction upon it.

163 U.S. 537 (1896), at p. 551.

asymmetrical character of segregation. Perhaps only a diagnosis in terms of inequality can do that.

There are a number of good responses available to this objection. First, the asymmetrical character of the injustices perpetuated by segregation can be at least partially accounted for by emphasizing that segregation was a system of *unequal* basic liberties. Of the five areas of liberty discussed above, in four of them the main complaint against segregation was that it created a system of unequal liberties (movement, residence, occupation, and political participation). Second, these unequal liberties resulted in inequality of opportunity. The same barriers that created unequal liberties also created unequal opportunities for movement, education, and employment. Although equal opportunity is not the same ideal, in my opinion, as the ideal of equal liberty, the two ideals do work in tandem to explain how segregation wronged African-Americans. Finally, the message sent by the imposition of a system of segregation and unequal basic liberties was deeply insulting to blacks and flattering to whites. Segregation was based on the belief that blacks, in contrast to whites, had negative characteristics that made them unworthy of equal basic liberties. As John Rawls has emphasized, denial of equal basic liberties to a person or group is deeply insulting and especially harmful to self-respect.[23] Segregation's unequal liberties were wrong not just in the greater restrictions they imposed on blacks, but also in the deep insult that they conveyed. As Joel Williamson put it:

> Separation also facilitated the subordination of the inferior race by constantly reminding the Negro that he lived in a world in which the white man was dominant, and in which the non-white was steadfastly denied access to the higher caste. Further, the impression of Negro inferiority would be constantly re-enforced by relegating the baser element, whenever possible, to the use of inferior facilities.[24]

---

[23] Rawls is worth quoting on this point:

> [S]elf-respect is most effectively encouraged and supported by the two principles of justice, . . . precisely because of the insistence on the equal basic liberties and the priority assigned them . . . The importance of self-respect is that it provides a secure sense of our own value, a firm conviction that our determinate conception of the good is worth carrying out. Without self-respect nothing may seem worth doing, and if some things have value for us, we may lack the will to pursue them.

"The Basic Liberties and Their Priority," *Political Liberalism*, p. 318.

[24] Joel Williamson, *After Slavery*, p. 276.

## III. CONTEMPORARY SEGREGATION AND LIBERTY

The United States is still in a segregated country three decades after the demise of legally authorized segregation. Separation between blacks and whites continues to be substantial in housing, where at least half of African-Americans still live in largely-black neighborhoods;[25] in schools, where housing segregation causes many African-American children to attend largely-black schools; in churches, where integration is extremely limited; and in social networks, where association between blacks and whites outside of the workplace is still limited.

Ongoing segregation is perpetuated by many factors. First, there is what we might call inertia, the adherence of both blacks and whites to patterns of living that were established during the Jim Crow era. In some cases we might describe this as loyalty, as when African-Americans continue to value and support their historic churches and colleges. But in many areas inertia is just a matter of people doing what they and their families have always done – and in the case of most whites that means keeping separate from blacks. Second, ongoing segregation is promoted by the on-average lower levels of income of blacks than whites, which make it harder for black families to move to new neighborhoods and to put their children in integrated private schools. Third, segregation is perpetuated by ongoing discrimination, especially in housing[26] and

---

[25] See Douglas S. Massey and Nancy A. Denton, *American Apartheid: Segregation and the Making of the Underclass* (Philadelphia: University of Pennsylvania Press, 1993).

[26] See Alex M. Johnson, Jr., "How Race and Poverty Intersect to Prevent Integration: Destabilizing Race as a Vehicle to Integrate Neighborhoods," *University of Pennsylvania Law Review* **143** (1995): 1595–1658. Johnson suggests four causes of residential segregation: (1) "racism no doubt continues to exist and to cause whites to resist living with or around Blacks in integrated neighborhoods" (p. 1609); (2) "the outward flight of whites to suburbia . . . is clearly a factor in maintaining residential segregation patterns in an era in which overt racism has diminished and lost favor" (p. 1611); (3) "the existence of government and private lender policies that discriminate against Blacks in the residential housing market in such a way as to restrict Blacks' choice of housing locales" (p. 1611); and (4) "poverty" (p. 1614). See also Michael H. Schill and Susan M. Wachter, "The Spatial Bias of Federal Housing Law and Policy: Concentrated Poverty in Urban America," *University of Pennsylvania Law Review* **143** (1995): 1285–1342.

employment.[27] Although such discrimination is illegal, there is no doubt whatever that it continues at a substantial level. In housing, African-Americans face discrimination when they try to rent as well as when they try to buy. Realtors often don't take blacks to see housing that is for rent or sale in white areas, and landlords often refuse to rent to blacks. In some all-white neighborhoods, blacks still face hostility and even violence from their new neighbors when they move in. A fourth factor follows from the third. Experiencing discrimination and hostility is extremely unpleasant, and a psychological aversion to facing it yet again surely causes many blacks to remain within largely-black neighborhoods and institutions.

Segregation is still supported by restrictions on basic liberties. Legally-authorized segregation and discrimination are gone, so there are no longer legal barriers to free association, movement, residence, or choice of employment. But there are still social strong barriers in these areas. These include ongoing discrimination in housing and employment, and violence against blacks who attempt to integrate white neighborhoods. Ongoing segregation has components that continue to infringe the basic liberties of African-Americans. Today's segregation is often described as "de facto" rather than "de jure," but this is misleading if it is taken to mean that segregation is no longer actively supported by the discrimination. And the active maintenance of barriers in housing and employment still delivers the insulting message that whites believe that African-Americans are unworthy of association with them and their children.

## IV. CONCLUSION

Even if we stick with a largely negative conception of liberty, as I have in my analysis, we find that both historic and contemporary segregation involve significant infringements of equal basic liberties. The ideal of equal basic liberties supports a powerful indictment of

[27] On employment discrimination and stereotypes see Joleen Kirschenman and Kathryn M. Neckerman, " 'We'd Love to Hire Them, but . . . ': The Meaning of Race for Employers," in Christopher Jencks and Paul E. Peterson, eds. *The Urban Underclass* (1991), Washington, D.C.: Brookings Institution, 1991, pp. 203–232.

both historic and contemporary segregation. When applied to racial segregation in the United States, the rhetoric of liberty has real substance.

Department of Philosophy
The University of Colorado
Boulder, CO 80309-0232 U.S.A.

FREDERICK SCHAUER

# GENERALITY AND EQUALITY

## I.

One hundred years ago the Supreme Court of the United States decided the case of *Plessy v. Ferguson*,[1] which held, notoriously, that a state mandate of racially separate public facilities (in this case, railroad cars) did not for that reason violate the Equal Protection Clause of the Fourteenth Amendment. In reaching this conclusion, the Court, even more notoriously, refused to accept the contention that social background conditions might render the superficially equal unequal in reality. "We consider the underlying fallacy of the plaintiff's argument to consist in the assumption that the enforced separation of the two races stamps the colored race with a badge of inferiority. If this be so, it is not by reason of anything found in the act, but solely because the colored race chooses to put that construction upon it. The argument necessarily assumes that if, as has been more than once the case and is not unlikely to be so again, the colored race should become the dominant power in the state legislature, and should enact a law in precisely similar terms, it would thereby relegate the white race to an inferior position. We imagine that the white race, at least, would not acquiesce in that assumption."[2]

This statement, of course, no longer represents American law. Of some relevance, obviously, is *Brown v. Board of Education*,[3] but its relevance to the central question in *Plessy* is easy to overstate. Although *Brown* held that racially segregated public school systems violated the Fourteenth Amendment, and that any contrary suggestions in *Plessy* could no longer be considered good law, the Court's

[1] 163 U.S. 537 (1896).
[2] 163 U.S. at 546.
[3] 347 U.S. 483 (1954).

*G. J. Postema (ed.), Racism and the Law: The Legacy and Lessons of Plessy,* 59–77.

conclusions in *Brown* were based on school-specific empirical findings about the impossibility of equal education under conditions of state-imposed racial segregation. In holding that "separate but equal is inherently unequal" in the context of public education, the Court left open the possibility that education was different, and that in other contexts *Plessy* might survive. If one defines effectiveness of travel in terms of the speed with which one gets from point *A* to point *B*, then it is not so clear that separate but equal is inherently unequal in the context of segregated railway cars, nor is it clear that empirical findings about educational effectiveness could transfer to claims about transportation effectiveness.

This possibility was short-lived. A year later, and essentially without opinion, the Supreme Court invalidated state-segregated buses,[4] as well as golf courses,[5] beaches, and bathhouses.[6] In doing so the Court severed the unconstitutionality of separate but physically equal public facilities from the empirical conclusions about the effect of segregation on equal educational opportunity, and in so doing made it clear that the central claim of *Plessy* had been definitively repudiated.

Yet if separate is now inherently unequal in golf courses and swimming pools as well as in schools, why is this so? Is it because separation is always irrational, and thus necessarily a reflection of an unjustified prejudice? But if separation is wrong because it is irrational, then the concept of equality appears to be doing no work, since we already have the non-equality-based conceptual resources to condemn any irrational governmental action, such as hiring as police officers only those born on dates including the number 5, or providing public housing only to those whose last names contain seven or fewer letters? Moreover, if the wrong of racial discrimination lies in its irrationality, then what is wrong with a high school that restricts its African-American musicians to the jazz ensemble, and restricts its white musicians to the baroque chamber orchestra, assuming that that distinction has more statistical reliability than the assumption that people born on a date including the number 5 will make better police officers than those with other birthdays? One

[4] *Gayle v. Browder*, 352 U.S. 903 (1956).
[5] *Holmes v. City of Atlanta*, 350 U.S. 879 (1955).
[6] *Mayor of Baltimore v. Dawson*, 350 U.S. 877 (1955).

possible answer is that the distinction, even if non-spurious in the statistical sense, is unjust because, after all, there are African-American baroque musicians and white jazz musicians. Basing a total separation on a statistically relevant but imperfect distinction, it might be argued, is unjust just because of its imperfection. Analyzing this possibility, that the injustices that we often characterize as inequalities are centrally about the use of imperfect generalizations, is my primary goal in this paper. Thus my aim is to examine the question of *generality*, since people often assume that the root of inequality lies in generalizing about people, and that the falsity (and thus the irrationality) of such generalizations explains our social and legal judgments of inequality. My goal here is modest. It is not to offer an account of equality. Rather, it is to offer an analysis of one possible root for a judgment of inequality. If, as I shall argue, this root will not sustain the concept of equality (and inequality) as we know it, then it is not that the concept of equality is flawed. It is only that one pervasive understanding of its basis is flawed, and that the search for a sound basis must start elsewhere than in the concept of imprecise generalization.

## II.

The category at issue in *Plessy* was the category of race, and if it is unjust to separate people by race, the injustice must lie either in something about race as a category, or something about categorization as such. Either it is wrong to use race as a socially relevant category because of the characteristics of the category of race, or it is wrong to engage in a certain kind of categorial generalization, with race being but an instantiation of the larger problem. My goal is to separate these possibilities, so I will focus on generalization itself, independent of the presence of potentially morally special categories, such as race, gender, or sexual orientation.

Consider the typical scenario in which a newspaper or government agency publishes a report exposing wrongdoing by auto mechanics. Or perhaps the wrongs have been committed by funeral directors, car salesmen, lawyers, surgeons, civil servants, or stockbrokers. The report charges that auto mechanics routinely make unnecessary repairs, that surgeons perform unnecessary operations, that funeral directors exploit the bereaved, that civil servants perform personal tasks with government resources, or that members of some other profession regularly overcharge their customers, perform shoddy work, commit malpractice, or engage in fraudulent practices. The next day we hear the expected response from the president of the National Association of Auto Mechanics or its equivalent for funeral directors, stockbrokers, lawyers, surgeons, civil servants, or car salesmen. The report is unfair, the president tells us, because not *all* auto mechanics/funeral directors/stockbrokers/lawyers/surgeons/civil servants/car salesmen engage in the questionable practices. Although *some* do, the president admits (the evidence typically being too overwhelming to make any other response plausible), these cases are the exception and not the rule, and the Association is doing everything in its power to deal with the small minority of individuals who are giving the profession a bad name. In fact, the Association has just put into place new regulations and enforcement mechanisms designed to guarantee that the few bad apples who are giving all of the honest members of the profession a bad name are punished severely and promptly.

We typically treat such protestations of unfairness with the cynicism they deserve, but the claim on behalf of the allegedly aggrieved profession nevertheless resonates with many people. Even if 40% of the dealers in used automobiles turn back odometers in order to make their products look newer than they are, there remain 60% who do not engage in the fraudulent practice, yet suffer from the stigma created by the other 40%. Upon learning that 40% of the members of a profession are corrupt, few of us would resist looking askance at 100% of that profession, including the 60% who had done nothing wrong. Moreover, few of us could avoid taking into account these figures in making concrete decisions that affect our lives. Most of us, I suspect, would be more reluctant to retain as an investment advisor a person who had previously been a seller of used cars than one who had previously been a social worker. Yet as we do this, we worry, because we are doing just what makes plausible the complaint of unfairness on the part of the impugned profession. We are attributing to all the sins of the few, and we are torn by conflicting feelings because such attributions seem simultaneously rational and unfair.

When we stigmatize an entire profession because of the behavior of some of its members, or when we engage in similar attributions in other areas of decision-making, we undertake a process of generalization. "Painting with a broad brush," the slightly pejorative expression puts it. From the existence of a property within some or many, but not all, members of a class, we make statements and decisions with respect to the entire class. Not all, and not even most, airline pilots suffer decreased alertness when they pass the age of 60, yet all commercial pilots must retire at that age. When a young male acquires a driver's license, his family's insurance premiums will rise dramatically, even if *their* son is the paragon of caution less likely to be involved in an accident than most adults. When a particular breed of dog, notably the pit bull terrier,[7] is shown to have a higher incidence of violent behavior than other breeds, there are moves to outlaw the breed itself, even in the face of claims that such an action would be unfair to the vast majority of pit bulls (or their owners) no more likely to be dangerous than any other dog.

It is routine, therefore, that we make decisions based on generalizations, on probabilities, on tendencies. It is not only the insurance industry which operates actuarially, but all of us, with more frequency than we often recognize. Yet in engaging in actuarial decision-making – in making decisions with respect to all members of a class because of what is true about only some or most members of that class – we make decisions that with respect to individual cases seem wrong. Every alert pilot forced to retire upon reaching the age of 60, every safe driver whose insurance rates rise because of the category within which she is placed, every docile put bull put down or separated from its owner, and every honest auto mechanic who must endure the suspicions of customers and the burden of intrusive regulation represents a mistake in some sense. Through no fault of their own, innocent people have been swept up in the category within

[7] See City of Cincinnati, Ordinance No. 43 of 1987, amending the Cincinnati Municipal Code to provide that "No person shall own, keep, or harbor a pit bull terrier . . . within the municipal limits of Cincinnati." The ordinance makes clear that the basis for the total prohibition is "certain vicious characteristics" of the breed. The relevant contrast is with the typical "vicious dog" or "dangerous dog" ordinance, which is not breed-specific. See, for example, Chapter 3, Article 2, Section 210 of the Municipal Code of Lawrence, Kansas, whose definition of a "vicious dog" is with reference to a specific dog and not to a breed.

which they are placed. When we paint with a broad brush, we lose the ability to draw the fine distinctions that strike us as both real and important.

From a utilitarian perspective, the problem of generality in decision-making is no problem at all. For the utilitarian, we should have no regret that a utility-maximizing maximizing decision procedure might paint with a broad brush and so produce consequences for individuals that from a non-utilitarian perspective they do not "deserve." Under a utilitarian approach, the inaccuracy of painting with a broad brush is but another action to be evaluated according to its net consequences.[8] Yet the centrality of the question of punishing the innocent in debates between utilitarians and their opponents demonstrates just how persistent is the worry that animates the resistance to actuarial decision-making.[9] And some of this worry carries over to the question of equality, with the perceived injustice of refusing to look at people individually being at the heart both of the flaws of generalized decision-making and of the vice of inequality. If inequality itself is also no problem for the utilitarian (except insofar as the basic insight of utilitarianism – that each counts for one and no one more than one – is itself equality-based,[10] then it should come as no surprise that actuarial decision-making is no problem for the utilitarian. But if, *contra* unalloyed utilitarianism, inequality is a problem for many people, is it a problem for the same non-utilitarian reason that actuarial decision-making is a problem for many people?

## III.

The distinction between what is true generally for a class and what is true for each member of that class generates a tension that has been recognized since classical times. Consider the dialogue in Plato's

---

[8] See, for example, Louis Kaplow, "The Value of Accuracy in Adjudication," Harvard Law School Program in Law and Economics Discussion Paper No. 123, March, 1993.

[9] For a good overview, see Alan Wertheimer, "Punishing the Innocent – Unintentionally," *Inquiry* **20** (1978): 45–65.

[10] For discussion, see James Steintrager, *Bentham* (Ithaca, New York: Cornell University Press, 1977), pp. 29–31, 57.

*Statesman.*[11] Here the Eleatic Stranger observes that "the endless irregular movements of human things, do not admit of any universal and simple rule." Yet the Stranger recognizes that "the legislator who has to preside over the herd . . . will lay down laws in general form for the majority, roughly meeting the cases of individuals." But here the "roughly" is key, for Plato's argument proceeds to the conclusion that when there is an opportunity to avoid the error caused by the application of the universal and simple rule to some particular case, it would be "evil," a "disgrace," and an "injustice" not to do so. Indeed, the examples Plato uses to make the claim of injustice are intriguing. In the voice of the Stranger, Plato asks us to consider the "training-master," not unlike today's personal trainer, and a physician. Suppose the training master and the physician must be away, and leave instructions for the regimen to be followed by their charges in their absence. Yet if the training-master or the physician should return sooner than expected, Plato argues, and if it should appear upon their return that the prescribed regimen did not *then* strike them as best at *that* time, "nothing would be more unjust" than for them to refuse to make the necessary modification.

By maintaining that the regimen should be modified in light of subsequent information, Plato might be understood simply to be making the point that rules made at one time might at a later time seem suboptimal, and that the rules should be modified, or updated, if it is at all possible to do so. This point, familiar in the American literature of statutory interpretation,[12] is about the limitations of human foresight, about the fact that rules necessarily prescribe for the future, that any estimation of future consequences is beset by uncertainty, and that rules thus contain the conditions of their own obsolescence.

Yet the possibility that good rules made at one time might seem poor ones later is not Plato's concern. For Plato the return of the training master is the occasion not for the training master to update a

[11] Edith Hamilton and Huntington Cairns, eds., *Plato: The Collected Dialogues* (Princeton: Princeton University Press, 1961), pp. 1018–85.

[12] See, for example, Guido Calabresi, *A Common Law for the Age of Statutes* (Cambridge: Harvard University Press, 1982); William N. Eskridge, Jr., *Dynamic Statutory Interpretation* (Cambridge: Harvard University Press, 1994); Cass Sunstein, "Interpreting Statutes in the Regulatory State," *Harvard Law Review* **103** (1989): 405–505.

general regimen, but rather to question the necessity of a prescribed regimen at all. The regimen, after all, is itself general. That is what a regimen is. For Plato the departure of the training master on a journey necessitates the prescription of a general regimen, as opposed to the giving of more particularized and continuous advice. When the training master returns, the regimen is no longer necessary, and the fact that the training master abandons the regimen is not a point about the obsolescence of the regimen, but about the fact that regimens themselves are subject by virtue of their generality to the possibility of being mistaken in individual cases.

Plato's characterization of the training master's error as an "injustice," however, is curious. We know, as Plato knew, that general rules may be in error, where the notion of an error is defined either in terms of serving the background purpose or rationale of the rule,[13] or in terms of what the rule-maker would have done, in person, had she confronted this individual case in the absence of any rule. So we can think of the fit 60 year-old pilot forced to retire for reasons of actuarial unfitness as an error, just as we can think of the stigma attached to the honest car salesman as an error. If the purpose of the prohibition on pit bulls is to decrease the incidence of dangerous dogs, and if the omniscient regulator would eliminate all dogs that are dangerous (many of which are not pit bulls) and none that are not (many of which are pit bulls), then every non-dangerous pit bull swept up in the broad prohibition of all pit bulls is an error. So too is it an error in the same sense when a family's insurance premiums escalate dramatically because their son has reached driving age, even if this particular sixteen year old boy is more cautious than most adults. Yet in describing cases like these as cases of *injustice*, Plato suggests that something is morally amiss when we refuse to correct the general to take account of the particular. Plato is right in reminding us that reliance on general rules necessarily contains the possibility of error in individual cases. But it is far from self-evident that every failure to correct such an error is an injustice, and it is not clear what conception of justice and injustice produces this conclusion.

---

[13] I explore all of this at great length in Frederick Schauer, *Playing By the Rules: A Philosophical Examination of Rule-Based Decision-Making in Law and in Life* (Oxford: Clarendon Press, 1991).

We see the same claim in the *Nichomachean Ethics*, where Aristotle gives us "a digression on equity, which corrects the deficiencies of legal justice."[14] Here Aristotle uses the word "justice" in a different sense, for he is talking about "legal justice," by his definition the act of following the rules as laid down in the formal law. But as with Plato in the *Statesman*, Aristotle recognizes that "there are some things about which it is not possible to pronounce rightly in general terms." He sees that it is often "necessary to make a general pronouncement," and that in doing so "the law takes account of the majority of cases." But this will inevitably produce errors, although "the error lies not in the law or in the legislator, but in the nature of the case; for the raw material of human behavior is essentially of this kind." When such errors arise, Aristotle maintains, it is necessary to resort to *equity* to correct "the error due to generalization... This is the essential nature of equity; it is a rectification of the law in so far as the law is defective on account of its generality."

Again Aristotle does not tell us why he believes that such correction is morally *necessary*, but he follows Plato in believing it demanded by justice. Equity, correcting the error of generality to reach the right result in the individual case, is to Aristotle "superior" to the "legal justice" that consists entirely in the following of the formal rules. "This is why equity, although just, and better than a kind of justice, is not better than absolute justice." "Equity is just, but not what is legally just: it is a rectification of legal justice."

The language of "rectification," and the argument of its necessity, makes Aristotle's argument coincide with Plato's. When we see a case in which the generality of a rule has produced a result different from the result that would have been produced by the "legislator himself ... if he had been aware of the [particular] circumstances," it is for Aristotle a moral necessity to make the correction. Failure to do so is an injustice, one that Aristotle sees as an inappropriate

---

[14] *Nichomachean Ethics* 1137b. Also relevant is *Rhetoric* 1374 and *Rhetoric* 1394. For useful commentary, see Georgios Anagnostopoulos, *Aristotle on the Goals and Exactness of Ethics* (Berkeley: University of California Press, 1994); Bernard Yack, *The Problems of a Political Animal: Community, Justice, and Conflict in Aristotelian Political Thought* (Berkeley: University of California Press, 1993), pp. 175–208; Roger A. Shiner, "Aristotle's Theory of Equity," *Loyola of Los Angeles Law Review* **27** (1994): 1245–64.

elevation of a kind of justice, legal justice, above what he calls "absolute justice," getting the right result in each and every case.

IV.

The basic analytic point made by Plato and Aristotle is evident: proceeding by general rule will at times produce outcomes different from and inferior to the outcomes that would be produced were the rule-makers themselves to address each case in its full particularity. Yet from this observation Plato and Aristotle proceed too quickly to the conclusion that correction is a moral necessity. For both of them the errors produced by the rigid application of rules stand as injustices to be corrected, and testimony to our own injustice if we refuse to do so. Both understood that justice might at times have to be sacrificed to efficiency. But we expect their acknowledgment would have been grudging. Perhaps, each would say, it is necessary to require all pilots to retire at the age of 60, and perhaps it is necessary to stigmatize all auto mechanics in order to protect us from the sins of some, but such actions should leave a distaste in our mouths and a moral residue in our calculations.

Yet why is it that when the training-master's general rules turn out not to be best for this person at this time in this place, and when the training-master refuses to modify them, he has acted unjustly? If we define injustice just *as* the failure to correct an error of generality, then the failure to correct is, by definition, an injustice. But for most of us an injustice is something bigger, or deeper. It is an error of a special kind – a moral error. I may feel frustrated when I, as an experienced and cautious driver, must even on a clear dry day obey the speed limits designed for those less experienced and cautious than me. But surely no injustice has been done to me, and no injustice has been done when, having stopped me for exceeding the speed limits, the police officer is not even interested in hearing about my skills as a driver or about the safety of today's driving conditions. If we take the case of the airline pilot and for a human being substitute an inanimate object, is the sense of unfairness the same? *Consumer Reports* generalizes about the reliability of different models of automobiles from past repair records, but the process is the same. If on the basis of *Consumer Reports* I refuse to buy a particular model, I have relied on a generalization, recognizing that in doing so I may have bought an unreliable token of a reliable type, and refrained from buying what might have turned out to be a reliable token of an unreliable type.

If it seems odd to think of my refusal to recognize the possibility of a reliable car within a statistically unreliable brand as a case of injustice – and it does for me – then it may be similarly odd to think of the training-master's possible refusal to withdraw the regimen or correct its errors as a case of injustice. It is true that the latter seems to have consequences for persons that the former does not, but it is odd to think of every inaccuracy with personal consequences as an injustice, especially once we recognize that every application of a rule *qua* rule entails the risk of just this kind of inaccuracy. Thus it appears as if there is a gap between error and injustice, and if this conclusion about the gap between injustice and error is correct, then it is no longer clear that categorial generalization is unjust simply because of the imprecision of the generalization, and thus no longer clear that categorial generalization is the wrong lying behind the concept of unjust discrimination.

## V.

I have focused on the necessary generality of rules, but the issue is not just about rules. Rules, by prescribing what is to be done for all of the class specified by the rule on the basis of what would be desirable for some or most of the class,[15] are but examples of probabilistic reasoning. The presupposition of a rule is that the category to which the rule attaches is statistically correlated with the production of the outcome that the rule directs. The generality of rules, therefore, is but an instantiation of the phenomenon of generality in decision-making.

Consider the debates about the use of probabilities in law. In the literature on this problem one of the canonical examples is a pared-down version of a real case,[16] the pared-down version usually

[15] It is common to think of the issue as arising when most but not all of a class contains the particular trait, but the notion of "most" is a bit of a red herring. Generalizing from a trait possessed by a minority of members of a class to the entirety of the class is a quite common and often actuarially justified approach.

[16] *Smith v. Rapid Transit*, 317 Mass. 469, 58 N.E.2d 754 (1945).

going by the name of the Blue Bus Problem.[17] Suppose you are knocked down by a bus at night, when it is too dark to identify either the particular bus or even the company that owns it. It turns out, however, that 60% of the buses in town are owned by the Blue Bus Company; and in a civil suit you need to prove your case only by a preponderance of the evidence, with anything over a 50% probability being sufficient for a plaintiff to recover against a defendant. So if in a typical accident case the judge or jury believes to a 51% probability that the plaintiff's account of the circumstances is true, the plaintiff will recover, even if the judge or jury believes to as much as a 49% probability that the defendant is telling the truth and the plaintiff is lying. Yet if this is true, then you ought to be able to recover against the Blue Bus Company, since (assuming there is no doubt that you have been hit by a bus) there is a 60% probability that you have been hit by one of their buses.

The academic literature on the Blue Bus and related problems is marked by a clash of competing intuitions. On one side are those who believe it would be manifestly unjust to find against the Blue Bus Company in the absence of any particularized evidence whatsoever that they have done anything wrong. And on the other side are those who think that there is no reason not to find against the Blue Bus Company in a case like this, where the plaintiff is 100% sure that it was a bus, and where there is a 60% chance that it was a Blue Bus Company bus, given that we would have no qualms at all in finding against the company where the plaintiff testified he was sure that it was a Blue Bus Company bus, but where the jury was only 60% sure the plaintiff was correct in making this identification. And on the sidelines stand the puzzled statisticians and decision theorists, wondering why the legal system in all such cases does not just award the plaintiff 60% of his damages and be done with it.

Yet in rejecting the statistician's obvious (to the statistician) solution, the law, with its statistically dubious all-or-nothing approach, is closer than we imagine to the way in which we use probabilities in a wide variety of decision-making contexts. When the insurance

[17] For examples of the voluminous literature, see Judith Jarvis Thomson, "Liability and Individualized Evidence," in *Rights, Restitution, and Risk*, William Parent, ed. (Cambridge, Massachusetts: Harvard University Press, 1986), pp. 225–50; Daniel Shaviro, "Statistical-Probability Evidence and the Appearance of Justice," *Harvard Law Review* **103** (1989): 530–54.

company raises the rates for all families with eighteen year old male drivers because of its experience with the class of eighteen year old male drivers, it is using that experience to assess the probability that a random member of that class will be involved in an accident. In raising the rates because of its probabilistic belief that the likelihood of an accident for a random member of this class is higher than that for a random member of most other classes of drivers, the insurance company is making an assessment divorced from all of the facts about a particular driver, just as awarding damages to the plaintiff against the Blue Bus Company strikes some people as penalizing the Blue Bus Company without sufficient evidence about the circumstances of *this* accident. Whether it be the stigmatization of the honest auto mechanic, or the compelled retirement of the fit airline pilot, or the financial burden on the safe driving eighteen year old, or the liability on the Blue Bus Company, probabilistic decision-making is all around us, even as worries about it are all around us as well.

Thus what appeared to be a problem about rules is in fact the problem of *categorial* reasoning.[18] When we make decisions on the basis of groups, classes, or categories, we necessarily ignore particulars in favor of tendencies, tendencies assessed on the basis of some collection of particulars. At times these collections will be collections of individual characteristics, as when we suppress the differences among pilots by making them all retire at the age of 60. And at times these collections will be collections of concrete events, as when the 55 mile per hour speed limit does not distinguish between day and night, wet or dry, sparse traffic or heavy. But whether the categorial compression of the diversity be a compression of differences among people or events, the effect is still to make decisions on the basis of a larger rather than smaller piece of the world. And a large part of what I maintain here, partly through pointing out the numerous

[18] *Categorial* is less familiar and less felicitous than *categorical*, and I use it in part just for that reason. "Categorical" carries suggestions of the absolute, the unyielding, and the non-overridable, as in, most famously, Kant's Categorical Imperative. For my purposes this is a side issue, for I am interested in the question of decision-making on the basis of large chunks of the world – categories – rather than the weight that those decisions will have. Put differently, I am more interested in the size than in the weight of our decisions, and the slightly jarring (and also more precise) "categorial" is a good reminder of this distinction.

areas in which just this form of decision-making is taken as a morally permissible commonplace, is that the errors of over-generalization are, themselves, a necessary part of human decision-making, and not evidence of injustice.

## VI.

Yet ignoring individual differences has a bad odor these days, and one reason for that is the way in which we commonly conceive the injustices of discrimination on the basis of race, gender, sexual orientation, ethnicity, disability, etc. Typically, and appropriately, we condemn the *stereotypes* that try to tell us that blacks are lazy, that women are flighty, that gay men lack courage, that Jews are dishonest. In condemning such stereotypes, we often urge that people be seen as individuals. We do not deny that there are lazy blacks and dishonest Jews, but there are also lazy Jews and dishonest blacks, just as there are lazy and dishonest members of any other class of human beings we can construct. If we could only characterize people for what *they* are, it is often said, rather than on the basis of their membership in some group, we could expunge much of the evil of discrimination that plagues us.

The typical claim about stereotyping, however, is ambiguous as between the statistically spurious attributions and the attributions that *do* have some statistical or actuarial soundness.[19] On the assumptions, which I believe well-founded, that African-Americans are no more likely to be lazy than a random sample of the population as a whole, and that Jews are no more likely to engage in sharp business practices than a random sample of the population, then the problem is not with stereotyping or generalization as such, but simply with the factually unfounded attribution of a characteristic to a group. The special problem of generalization and of categorial thinking is highlighted, however, in the context of those attributions that are not statistically spurious, and thus have some sound actuarial basis. Just as often as we condemn the spurious stereotypes, we condemn those stereotypes that *do* appear to have some statistical empirical basis, such as stereotypes based on the frailty of the elderly or the lack of

[19] See Yueh-Ting Lee, Lee J. Jussim, and Clark R. McCauley, *Stereotype Accuracy* (Washington, D.C.: American Psychological Association, 1995).

upper body strength among women. That there are more 55 year old pilots and lawyers than there are 55 year old linebackers is not simply evidence of invidious discrimination by the National Football League. Still, not *all* elderly people are weak, it is said, and to refuse to allow those who are not, on the basis of a generalization from those who are, is just what it is to discriminate unjustly. The goal of equality, consequently, often takes the form of the claim that individuals are entitled to be evaluated on their own characteristics, rather than on the basis of the characteristics, even if in some way statistically relevant, of a class into which society happens to put them. In this way, the claims for equality and the claims for particularity are commonly conjoined.

Yet equality itself may be the ultimate non-particular claim. "All men are created equal," the Declaration of Independence announces, and in so doing highlights the commonality among all human beings, even if unfortunately only aspirational, and suppresses the differences. Of course we are not all equal, in a descriptive sense, and it is just this denial of the similarity among people that has since Aristotle provided the purchase for claims about the injustice of treating as similar what is in fact different. Yet similarity and equality are plainly kin, and the justice of the *ascriptive* sense of "All men are created equally" even as we recognize the falsity of the descriptive sense reminds us of the fact that even the concept of equality itself embodies the tension between the claims of generality and of particularity.

The question has moved to the forefront as a result of two recent Supreme Court cases. Consider first Justice Ginsberg's opinion for the Court in *United States v. Virginia*,[20] holding unconstitutional the refusal to admit women to the Virginia Military Institute. The trial court, relying on expert testimony offered by the Commonwealth of Virginia, had concluded that there were "gender-based developmental differences" between men and women, that these differences reflected gender-based "tendencies" with respect to adaptability to a combative and adversarial educational environment, and that these differences, conceded by the witnesses to be non-universal, justified the all-male educational environment at the Virginia Military Institute.

[20] 116 S. Ct. 2264 (1996).

In response to these findings below, the United States argued that courts should take a " 'hard look' " at such "generalizations or 'tendencies,' " and that "[s]tate actors controlling gates to opportunity [may] not exclude qualified individuals based on 'fixed notions concerning the roles and abilities of males and females.' " This response suggests four importantly different possibilities. One is that the generalization or tendency was simply spurious, and its acceptance based on nothing but empirically unjustified prejudice, as with the claim, still widely accepted in France, that women can be good household cooks but lack the creativity to be serious chefs. Another is that the generalization or tendency is empirically non-spurious, but rather than being a justification *for* discrimination, is instead the consequence *of* it, as is almost certainly the case for gender-based differentials in tests for mathematical aptitude. A third is that the generalization is empirically sound, but is irrelevant to the job at hand, as with a test for upper body strength for computer programmers. And a fourth is that the generalization or tendency is empirically sound, is not a consequence of discrimination, is relevant to the job at hand, but still may not be used as a basis for avoiding individualized testing of or inquiry into the trait in question, as with, for example, excluding women by virtue of gender from jobs that genuinely do require a considerable amount of upper body strength.

Justice Ginsburg's opinion does not directly address these four possibilities, and much of her opinion is ambiguous as to whether VMI's justification failed because it was statistically spurious, statistically sound but itself an effect of previous discrimination, statistically sound but correlated only to an irrelevant qualification, or statistically sound but nevertheless morally and constitutionally impermissible. She does say at one point that "estimates of what is appropriate for most women . . . no longer justify denying the opportunity to women whose talent and capacity place them outside the average description," thus suggesting that statistical spuriousness is not the basis for the Court's decision, and this is consistent with earlier suggestions in *Craig v. Boren*[21] that the evil of gender dis-

[21] 429 U.S. 190 (1976). "Thus, if statistics were to govern the permissibility of state alcohol regulation without regard to the Equal Protection Clause as a limiting principle, it might follow that States could freely favor Jews and Italian Catholics at the expense of all other Americans, since available studies regularly demonstrate that the former two groups exhibit the lowest rates of problem drinking."

crimination does not exist because of such discrimination's statistical irrelevance, but despite its statistical relevance.

The point of this exploration is not to deal with the question of gender discrimination as such. Rather, it is to suggest that there is an important distinction – moral, legal, and constitutional – between identifying the evil of gender discrimination as having something to do with what is wrong with *gender* discrimination *qua* gender discrimination (and so too for discrimination on the basis of race) or instead with gender discrimination being merely an instantiation of a larger point about a putative pervasive evil of not allowing individuals to make individualized claims relating to their own circumstances when they find themselves as outliers in a statistically non-spurious category. To rephrase the question, is it appropriate to generalize from the evil of gender discrimination to the evil of all other forms of classification in which individuals, as with the women who could succeed at VMI as now structured, find themselves as mischaracterized members of a larger but not (necessarily) misdescribed class? And the implication of my argument above is that treating non-individualized decision-making as the morally relevant category, and gender discrimination as but its instantiation, is inconsistent with our acceptance of non-individualized decision-making in numerous other areas, and inconsistent as well with the perception that gender discrimination is not unjust because it is irrelevant, but is unjust even when it *is* relevant.

The importance of the issue is underscored by the fact that the same issue lurks in Justice Kennedy's opinion for the Supreme Court in *Romer v. Evans*,[22] is highlighted in Justice Scalia's dissent in the same case, and is much more on the surface in much recent litigation regarding discrimination against gays and lesbians, especially the litigation regarding gays and lesbians in the military.[23] Assuming that it would be constitutionally permissible to discriminate against those who engage in homosexual *conduct* as long as *Bowers v. Hardwick*[24] remains on the books,[25] the issue is whether a restriction on

22 116 S. Ct. 1620 (1996).

23 See, for example, *Cammermeyer v. Aspin*, 850 F. Supp. 910 (W.D. Wash. 1994); *Dahl v. Secretary of the Navy*, 830 F. Supp. 1319 (E.D. Cal. 1993).

24 478 U.S. 186 (1986).

25 In case any reader is interested, not only do I think *Bowers* morally and constitutionally wrong, but I also think it is sufficiently so as to morally justify

homosexual orientation, plainly correlated with homosexual conduct albeit at something less than 1.0, is impermissible precisely because of its over-inclusion, its willingness to assume for the entire class what is true for only part of it. Assuming there is no free speech issue (as there is when speech is the method of discovering an orientation not manifested in conduct), the issue here fits closely with that in the VMI case. If discrimination on the basis of sexual orientation is, *Bowers* notwithstanding, suspect or almost so, then the existence of a statistically relevant tendency is of no moment. But if neither the prohibition of homosexual conduct nor discrimination on the basis of sexual orientation is independently unconstitutional, then the issue presented is whether the existence of the generalization is itself sufficient to create a constitutional problem in its own right.

This should recall the brief history of the constitutional doctrine of irrebuttable presumptions.[26] For a few years, the Supreme Court seemed to believe that classificatory legislation that did not allow individuals about whom the classificatory presumption did not obtain to demonstrate their own "exception" was for that reason a deprivation of liberty or due process in violation of the Fourteenth Amendment, and was for that reason "arbitrary." The doctrine did not last very long,[27] seemingly because of the power of the argument, consistent with what I have argued here, that an irrebuttable presumption was in an important way a feature of all rules and therefore of all legislation.[28]

Which brings us back to the issue of stereotypes and generalizations. If statistically imprecise generalizations are not wrong for that reason alone, even in the area of their imprecision, then what is it that is *wrong* with a stereotype based on race, gender, or sexual orientation? If the wrong lies in the realm of statistical spuriousness, then we are at a loss to explain why racial separation is wrong when it is not

---

writing a doctrinally disingenuous decision in order to get around it, assuming a doctrinally honest decision would not have secured the requisite number of votes.

[26] *United States Department of Agriculture v. Murry*, 413 U.S. 508 (1973); *Cleveland Board of Education v. LaFleur*, 414 U.S. 632 (1974).

[27] See *Weinberger v. Salfi*, 422 U.S. 749 (1975); *Mourning v. Family Publications Service*, 411 U.S. 356 (1973); *Marshall v. United States*, 414 U.S. 417 (1974).

[28] See Note, "The Irrebuttable Presumption Doctrine in the Supreme Court," *Harvard Law Review* **87** (1974): 1534–56; Note, "Irrebuttable Presumptions: An Illusory Analysis," *Stanford Law Review* **27** (1975): 449–77.

spurious. And if the wrong does not lie in the realm of statistical spuriousness, and if, as we have seen, it does not lie either in the realm of non-spurious statistical imprecision, then it is something about race itself that is important, and so too for those other areas in which we believe, properly, that separation is wrong even when it is statistically non-spurious. But now that we have seen that statistical imprecision cannot be the answer, we have made progress toward identifying the factors that make unjust discrimination unjust. That discrimination is imprecise is a temptingly easy answer, but it turns out that it is also a wrong one. The search for the right one must lie not in the realm of the goal of treating every person as an individual, for that turns out to be a weaker moral norm than many people suppose. Rather, the answer likely lies in the realm of the history of racial generalization, in the historical overuse of such generalizations, and in a morally mandated underuse as a check on the possibility of overuse. If this is right, it explains why imprecise but non-spurious generalizations are permissible in a broad range of decisions, but impermissible for certain categories. Further exploration of this possibility, however, must be left for another occasion.[29]

John F. Kennedy School of Government
Harvard University
Cambridge, MA 02138 U.S.A.

[29] For helpful comments, I am grateful to Elizabeth Garrett, Mary Mahowald, Nicholas White, and audiences at New York University and the University of Chicago.

BERNARD R. BOXILL

# WASHINGTON, DU BOIS AND *PLESSY V. FERGUSON*

When Homer Plessy brought suit against the state of Louisiana for its laws segregating the races on railways he was not complaining about the poor accommodations for black people on the state's railways. Neither was he objecting to the economic injustice of forcing blacks to pay the same fare as whites, but for inferior accommodations. If the state required the railways to reserve separate accommodations for black people that were as good as the accommodations they reserved for white people this would have satisfied Booker T. Washington – he said so – but it would not have satisfied Plessy.[1] Plessy would not be satisfied until he got the right to sit next to whites on railway carriages.

The Court rejected his suit. The premise of the Louisiana statute upheld by the Court was not an objection to blacks being in close physical proximity to whites. In the late 19th century in the South, blacks were often in close proximity to whites as servants and subordinates. But if racial segregation on railways was abolished, blacks would be in close proximity to whites as fellow travellers and citizens, and consequently would be in circumstances where they could meet whites on terms approaching equality. It was the demand to be allowed to be in such circumstances with whites in Plessy's suit that the Court rejected, calling it a demand for "social equality," and implying that in seeking such equality Plessy was asking that blacks have the right to force their company on people who did not want it.[2] The Court was mistaken. Plessy wanted the right to sit next to whites as an equal, but to sit next to someone, even as an equal, is not to force your company on him. Keeping company with others involves

---

[1] Booker T. Washington, Letter to the Editor, *Montgomery Adviser*, April 30, 1885, in *African American Political Thought 1890–1930*, edited by Cary D. Wintz (New York: M. E. Sharp, 1996), p. 21.

[2] *Plessy v. Ferguson*, 163 U.S. 537 (1896). All references to this case are drawn from *Civil Rights: Leading Cases*, edited by Derrick A. Bell Jr. (Boston: Little, Brown and Co., 1980), p. 71.

*G. J. Postema (ed.), Racism and the Law: The Legacy and Lessons of Plessy,* 79–110.

conversing with them, and people can sit next to each other as equals and never converse. But the charge that Plessy was seeking "social equality," and the right to force his company on those who did not want it, was an effective diversionary strategy that segregationists had often exploited before, and they continued to use it long after *Plessy*. In 1921, W.E.B. Du Bois described it as an "undeceiving deception" that had gone on for fifty years. As he put it, the white man asked the Negro, "Do you want Social Equality?" and the Negro answered with "an emphatic and indignant No," meaning that he did not want to force his company on persons who did not want it. But, Du Bois continued, the Negro knew that "he was not answering the question the white man intended to ask," which was, "Do you mean to say that you consider yourself fit to associate with white people?" and the white man "knew that the Negro knew this, and that he himself had purposely asked a question of double and irreconcilable meaning . . ."[3]

Still, people who sit next to each other as equals are liable to begin to converse and then to associate with each other as equals. Since conversation and association with others are important opportunities for learning and material progress, this may suggest that Plessy's main argument against racial segregation was that it denied blacks these opportunities. For example, one of the arguments against segregated schools in the disputes that followed *Brown*, decided fifty-eight years after *Plessy*, was that black children were harmed by their isolation, and would learn from their white schoolmates, and advance more rapidly if schools were integrated. But Plessy's main complaint against racial segregation was not that it denied blacks important opportunities for education and advancement, but, rather, that it put a "badge of inferiority" on him.[4]

The Court replied that this complaint was groundless. It did not mean only that segregation laws were not intended as an insult to blacks; as Edmund Cahn noted in 1955, such an excuse comes too late when it is made after blacks inform lawmakers that segregation

---

[3] W. E. B. Du Bois, "President Harding and Social Equality," in *W. E. B. Du Bois: Writings*, edited by Nathan Huggins (New York: The Library of America, 1986), p. 1191.

[4] Bell, *Civil Rights: Leading Cases*, p. 70.

laws insult them.[5] The Court meant that there was nothing in the segregation laws to justify Plessy's complaint that they stamped him with a badge of inferiority, and that if he felt that it did this was only because he chose to "put that construction upon it."[6] Charles L. Black commented that "The curves of callousness and stupidity intersect at their respective maxima," in that claim.[7] He thought that it was "subjectively obvious" that segregation offended against equality, though he went on to back up this view with familiar facts about the South, like its long history of offences against blacks, the fact that it was "actionable defamation in the South to call a white man a Negro," and that "Separate but equal" facilities were "almost never really equal."[8] Cahn himself thought that the matter needed even less argument. One "speaks in terms of the most familiar and universally accepted standards of right and wrong," he wrote, "when one remarks that racial segregation under government auspices inevitably inflicts humiliation."[9] But while Black and Cahn are right that *de jure* racial segregation is obviously insulting, a brief comment may help to show just why it is so insulting. Although individuals generally thrive when they are free and able to associate with whoever they please, some associations can be very harmful. Individuals may be corrupted if they fall in with a "bad crowd," or they may waste their time and talents consorting with frivolous and foolish people, and sometimes they put their trust in criminals. Since even these very real dangers are not normally sufficient to curtail individuals' rights to freedom of association, the lawmakers efforts to make it impossible for blacks to associate with whites said or insinuated that blacks were extraordinarily corrupting and contaminating, or at best, that they were foolish, frivolous, and untrustworthy. If this is correct, we can begin to appreciate why Plessy felt that racial segregation stamped him with a "badge of inferiority."

We can, however, distinguish two reasons why he might have thought it so important to protest what racial segregation said or

---

[5] Edmund Cahn, "Jurisprudence," *New York University Law Review* **30** (1955): 150–169, at p. 158.

[6] Bell, *Civil Rights: Leading Cases*, p. 71.

[7] Charles L. black, "The Lawfulness of the Segregation Cases," *The Yale Law Journal* **69** (1960): 421–430, at p. 422, fn. 8.

[8] Ibid, pp. 424–426.

[9] Cahn, "Jurisprudence," p. 159.

insinuated about him. The first is that the statement provided the moral ground for racial segregation and the other policies and practices that denied him important opportunities to learn and advance. The second is the statement's sheer offensiveness to black self-respect. It denied that blacks were even eligible to associate with whites, but a claim to be eligible to associate with others is, as W.E.B. Du Bois put it, "the very essence of self-respect and human equality and it carries with it no jot of arrogance or assumption – it is simply, *Homo sum*."[10] And Du Bois was right, assuming that a belief that one is fit for one's basic moral rights is a part of self-respect, and if the qualities that make one eligible to associate with others also help to make one fit for one's basic moral rights.

Racial segregation was arguably not only offensive to self-respect but also potentially harmful to it. Answering the double edged question whether he wanted "Social Equality," Du Bois answered, "Certainly I do. Every normal decent human being wants to associate with his fellowmen on terms of equality . . . We will surely never stultify our souls by seeking those who despise us, but equally we will refuse to lie and say that we wish to be despised . . . The despising of men, regardless of gift and character, is a cruel crime. Of course, we want it abolished. Of course, we want social equality and we know we will never be real men until we get it."[11] Du Bois's answer allows that he was offended and hurt by racial segregation's statement that he was ineligible to associate with whites as an equal, but it suggests more than that. His implication that despising others is a "cruel crime," and that we will never be "real men" until we are not despised, suggests that he thought the statement also threatened black self-respect; cruel crimes are not simply offensive, but also potentially harmful, and people do not cease to be real men just because others say or do things offensive to their self-respect, though they are sometimes described as less than "real men" if they lose their self-respect. And many have agreed with him. Some, like Cahn, think that the charge that racial segregation is "psychologically injurious" is as obvious as the charge that it is insulting.[12] Others have conducted experiments to prove that racial segregation

[10] Du Bois, "President Harding and Social Equality," p. 1191.
[11] W. E. B. Du Bois, "Social Equality," *The Crisis* **24**(1) (May 1922), p. 8.
[12] Cahn, "Jurisprudence," p. 159.

undermines self-respect; for example, Kenneth Clark's famous "doll experiments," used by the plaintiffs in *Brown v Board of Education*[13] to challenge the alleged equality of racially segregated schools. In these experiments, Kenneth Clark presented black and white dolls to black children in segregated schools, and asked them which dolls were "nice" and "looked like them." When the majority of the black children picked the white dolls, Clark inferred that racial segregation in schools gave black children a "negative image" of themselves.[14] If his inference was sound, the contempt that racial segregation expressed for blacks was not only offensive to their self-respect but also potentially harmful to it, and Du Bois was right that such contempt was a "cruel crime," given that no one can have a worthwhile and happy life if her self-respect is undermined.

The view that blacks should protest the offensiveness of racial segregation's statement about them reaches further than the view that they should protest the statement because it helps to justify restricting their opportunities; whites can continue to make statements offensive and presumably harmful to black self-respect even when they do not use them to justify restricting black opportunities. When Clark repeated his experiments later, he discovered that black children in desegregated schools even more frequently claimed that the white dolls were the "nice" dolls and "looked like them" than black children in segregated schools.[15] Critics argued that this second experiment weakened his claim that racial segregation harmed black children's self-respect, but Clark himself thought that it only showed that racial segregation was not the only way white society could insult blacks and undermine their self-respect.[16] Du Bois's view (probably it was Plessy's too) was that blacks should take issue with such statements, even when they were not used to justify restricting black opportunities; blacks should protest them in the courts of law if possible, and in the court of public opinion if they got no satisfaction from the law. It also seems to have been Du Bois's

---

[13] 347 U.S. 483 (1954).

[14] See Lino A. Graglia, *Disaster By Decree* (Ithaca: Cornell University Press, 1976), pp. 27, 28.

[15] Ibid.

[16] I have explored this question at greater length in *Blacks and Social Justice*, second edition (Lanham: Rowman and Littlefield, 1992), pp. 89–106.

view that if they did not do so, that is, if they allowed public insults to go unchallenged, they were liable to lose their self-respect.

Not everyone in the black community agreed with Plessy and Du Bois that the worst thing about racial segregation was what it said about blacks. As I have noted Washington's main objection to racial segregation on railways was that it made blacks pay the same fare as whites but for inferior accommodations. And in general he was less exercised by what racial segregation said about blacks than about the economic opportunities it denied them. His famous dictum, "In all things that are purely social we can be as separate as the fingers, yet one as the hand in all things essential to mutual progress," suggests that he probably objected to racially segregated railways because they eliminated an opportunity for mutual progress.[17] Washington's disagreement with Plessy and Du Bois about what was most wrong about racial segregation naturally led him to disagree with them about how blacks should respond to it. While they felt that blacks should take special issue with, and strenuously protest, the false and execrable things it said about them, he felt that blacks would do better to take advantage of the economic opportunities available to them to become prosperous and independent.

From Du Bois's point of view there were three main reasons why Washington might have taken this position: Washington might not have understand what racial segregation was saying about blacks; he might have understood this, but failed to see that it justified denying blacks the economic opportunities he desired for them; and he might not have felt how offensive and potentially harmful racial segregation was to black self-respect because he did not understand or value self-respect. Most commentators have supposed that Du Bois was clearly right and Washington clearly wrong. However, reflection on Jean-Jacques Rousseau's views on some of the consequences of inequality have persuaded me that the issue is more complicated. In the first section, I defend the view of Plessy and Du Bois that blacks must protest their wrongs, but I distinguish two kinds of protest, protest as challenge and protest as persuasion, and I suggest that only protest as challenge is clearly mandatory. In the second section,

---

[17] Booker T. Washington, "The Atlanta Exposition Address," in Wintz, *African American Political Thought 1890–1930*, p. 25. For a statement of the benefits of association, see Washington, "My View of Segregation Laws," same volume, pp. 78–81.

I argue further that in circumstances of gross inequality protest as persuasion is liable be morally compromised and to lead to a loss of the protesters' integrity. Finally, in the third section, I consider how Frederick Douglass might have drawn on the theory of moral motivation sketched in the previous section to argue that the weak can gain moral power to lessen the dangers of protest as persuasion, and I suggest that Martin Luther King's account of civil disobedience may rely on a similar argument.

## I

As I noted earlier, there are two main reasons why Plessy and Du Bois might have felt that blacks should strenuously protest the false and offensive statements racial segregation made about them. The first is that such statements helped justify racial segregation and the other policies that denied blacks opportunities. The second is that these statements were offensive and threatening to black self-respect. Let us begin with the second, and in particular, with the argument that whites endanger blacks' self-respect when they make statements offensive to it.

That argument may rely on the assumption that a person's self-respect depends on the good image that he has of himself, and that he cannot maintain this good image if others undermine it by saying bad things about him. If that assumption is true, then since statements offensive to black self-respect, for example, that blacks are not fit for basic moral rights, say bad things about blacks, such statements are likely to undermine black self-respect. I am not impressed with this argument. I am ready to be persuaded that it would be hard for a person to sustain his self-respect, if the whole world despised him. But surely no one needs the whole world's approval to sustain his self-respect. In particular, blacks do not need whites to approve of them to be able to sustain their self-respect. It seems enough if other blacks, who are likely to know them better than whites know them anyway, approve of them. But this consideration allows that blacks' self-respect could be endangered by the negative opinion of observers they believe to be reliable, and this should lead one to wonder whether Du Bois worried that white contempt could harm black self-respect because he worried that whites were more reliable observers of blacks than blacks were of themselves.[18] Rousseau's theory of the tendency of the weak in societies with large inequalities to "live only in the opinions of others" suggests that Du Bois might very well have worried in this way.

According to Rousseau, human beings become concerned with what others think of them as soon as they acquire "ideas of merit and beauty which produce sentiments of preference," judge and rate others according to these ideas, and realize that others are doing the same to them.[19] But he implied that this concern became the preoccupation he called "living only in the opinion of others" only after various inventions and developments brought about the "great revolution" that resulted in a division of labor, mutual dependence, and the production of large surpluses.[20] Such surpluses stirred the imagination of the participants and made them greedy, but some, through accident and luck, found themselves in positions that enabled them to keep a disproportionately large amount of the surplus produced, and being greedy they took advantage of their good fortune, strengthened their positions and consolidated their advantages, and as a result large inequalities began to develop in the society.[21] Then when the weaker realized their predicament, and understood that they could increase their chances of getting their necessities and conveniences if they pleased the stronger, their self-interest and greed moved them to try to please the stronger, and since they naturally wanted to know if they were succeeding, they begin to worry and to be generally preoccupied with what the stronger thought of them. Then, as the process deepened and became a habit, the weaker became so obsessed with the stronger's conception of them that they forgot to try to form

[18] It is also possible, of course, to suspect that Du Bois believed that blacks in general tended to believe that whites were better observers of blacks than blacks were of themselves, but exempted himself from the general tendency. However I do not see how Du Bois being black himself could have justified that view.

[19] "Discourse on the Origin and the Foundations of Inequality among Men," Part Two, in *Jean-Jacques Rousseau, The First and Second Discourses Together with the Replies to Critics, and the Essay on the Origin of Languages*, edited by Victor Gourevitch (New York: Harper Torchbooks, 1986), p. 175.

[20] Rousseau, "Discourse on Inequality," in Gourevitch, *Jean Jacques Rousseau*, p. 177.

[21] It is important to emphasize that Rousseau believed that inequality and not mere mutual dependence was necessary for life in others to develop. Rousseau worried about dependence because he believed that it tended to lead to inequality.

independent conceptions of themselves, consequently lost all confidence in their ability to do so, and finally, forming no conception of themselves for themselves, gained their conception of themselves only from the conception that the strong had of them. At this point, having derived even the "sentiment" of their "own existence" solely from the judgment of the strong, they could think that they fared well only when they thought that the images the strong had of them fared well, and in this sense they began to "live only in the opinions of" the strong.[22]

If this argument is at all persuasive, blacks in American society are likely to have a bad case of "life in others" – where the "others" are whites – for whites are able to keep a disproportionately large amount of the society's surplus for themselves, and to limit and deny blacks' access to necessities and conveniences. And blacks' predicament would only be exacerbated if, as seems to be the case, whites tend to despise blacks and to be extremely chary about allowing blacks such access. Accordingly, if Du Bois being black shared in the general malaise, it would not be surprising if he was preoccupied with what whites thought of him; assumed that whites were the most reliable observers of blacks; felt his self-respect threatened by white affronts because he derived his conception of himself from the way whites conceived of him; and believed that blacks' positive conception of each other had to be validated by whites' positive conception of blacks.

Du Bois's admirers may object that I misrepresent his thought. Probably they will claim that he would have dismissed the idea that he gained his conception of himself from whites' conception of him, and consequently that he did not believe that he had to persuade whites to think well of him in order to validate his good conception of himself. But the first part of this claim cannot be sustained. One of Du Bois's most famous lines, that the "American world . . . only lets him [the Negro] see himself through the revelation of the other world," says plainly enough that he believed that blacks, and presumably Du Bois too, gained a compelling conception of themselves from

[22] Rousseau, "Discourse on Inequality," in Gourevitch, *Jean Jacques Rousseau*, p. 199. Of course Rousseau thought that the strong also live in the weak. I take this up later.

they way whites conceived of them.[23] It may be objected that these lines do not say unambiguously that the only conception blacks have of themselves is the conception whites have of them since there are other ways to gain a conception of oneself than by "looking" at oneself – metaphorically, of course – and indeed that Du Bois implied that blacks have a second conception of themselves, one which they did not gain from the way whites conceived of them, when he claimed that they had a "double-consciousness," and thought of themselves as both Negro and American.[24] But this objection does not invalidate the argument that in Du Bois's view blacks gained their most compelling, if not their only, conception of themselves from the way whites conceived of them. This argument remains valid because Du Bois insists that blacks only "see" themselves the way whites see them, and because we gain our most compelling conception of things from what we see, although naturally that conception is often limited and superficial.[25] If I am right about this, it remains that blacks would be excessively and morbidly dependent on whites for their conception of themselves, even if they did not gain their only conception of themselves from the conception that whites had of them.

A second objection to my interpretation of Du Bois's position is that although he maintained that blacks would lose their self-respect if they failed to protest white affronts to it, this was not because he believed that the affronts they left unsilenced would cost them their self-respect, but because he believed that they were obligated to challenge such affronts, and that the dereliction of this obligation would cost them their self-respect. This argument is compatible with the claim that blacks gain a compelling conception of themselves from whites' conception of them; it could, for example, be

[23] W. E. B. Du Bois, "Of Our Spiritual Strivings," in *The Souls of Black Folk*, edited by John Edgar Wideman (New York: Vintage Books, 1990), p. 8. The next sentence which speaks of "always looking at oneself through the eyes of others," confirms my claim.

[24] That blacks have a second conception of themselves not gained from the way whites conceive of them does not follow only from the claim that they think of themselves as both Negro and American since they could gain this conception of themselves from the way whites conceive of them. The claim that blacks have a "double-consciousness," is essential.

[25] I have pursued these issues at greater length in "Du Bois on black Double-Consciousness," unpublished manuscript.

interpreted as saying that blacks must challenge affronts to their self-respect, or else either remain afflicted by a "double-consciousness," or lose all independent conception of themselves and consequently lose self-respect. More generally, since affronts to self-respect offend morality, and one is obligated to stand up for morality, it is probably a sound argument that people are obligated to challenge, and consequently to protest affronts to their self-respect.[26]

But to thus protest claims offensive to self-respect is not to try to persuade those who make such claims that they ought to take them back. It is simply a defiant oath of allegiance to morality that tends to sustain self-respect. Perhaps for different reasons Derrick Bell, who proclaims the "permanence of racism," and consequently must have little confidence in the power of protest to persuade, nevertheless insists that protesting "offending situations," may help to "rescue self-esteem." Those of us who "speak out," he writes, are "moved by a deep sense of the fragility of our self-worth," and by a "determination to protect our sense of who we are . . . "[27] Du Bois too understood that the whole point of protest was not to persuade: "even when bending to the inevitable," he once wrote, "we bend with unabated protest."[28] But Du Bois also endorsed protest in its persuasive sense; indeed, he spent a good part of his long life trying to persuade whites to think well of blacks.[29] Now, of course, Du Bois had reason to do this, other than the false idea that blacks had to gain the good opinion of whites in order to keep their self-respect. As I noted earlier, affronts to black self-respect, typically involved or rested on claims that were used to justify denying blacks economic and other opportunities. If so, it would seem to make good sense for Du Bois to try to persuade whites that they ought to take back their affronts to blacks. The view of the nationalists that blacks should try to become powerful enough to simply seize

[26] Thomas E. Hill, "Servility and Self-Respect," *The Monist* **57** (1973): 87–104.

[27] Derrick A. Bell, *Confronting Authority* (Boston: Beacon Press, 1994), pp. ix, x.

[28] W. E. B. Du Bois, "The Parting of the Ways," in *W.E.B. Du Bois*, edited by William M. Tuttle, Jr. (Englewood Cliffs, New Jersey: Prentice Hall, 1973), p. 43. The same point is made at greater length in "A Philosophy for 1913," same volume, pp. 108–9.

[29] He began, as social scientist, with presenting whites with the facts about blacks. Then when this seemed to fail, he became, in his words, "master of propaganda," as editor of *The Crisis*.

these opportunities would not be enough. A society will be unstable if the groups or individuals that compose it despise each other, even if they are careful not to violate each other's rights because they respect each others' power. Natural changes and human policies and inventions cause power to shift unpredictably, and groups that today exist in a kind of peaceful balance tomorrow may become oppressor and victim. Knowing this, they will distrust and fear each other, and their schemes and maneuverings to keep and maintain power will fill their society with fear and violence. Further, since white contempt for blacks is morally wrong, even when it cannot harm their self-respect or diminish their opportunities, arguably blacks should try to correct it, even in such circumstances. Indeed, perhaps the failure to do so could show contempt for whites. How can anyone feel that he has no obligation to correct expressions of contempt – malign even if ineffectual attacks on his self-respect – unless he feels that the source of these expressions of contempt is beyond redemption? Perhaps it was this consideration that moved Du Bois to write, "if others hate and despise us, very well. There may be little or nothing that we can do to change their attitude. But one thing we can do: we can refuse to hate and despise them or say that hatred and contempt are fine human habits."[30]

But these considerations do not unambiguously support Du Bois's insistence on protest as persuasion. For example, although it was clearly important to undermine the moral basis of policies that denied blacks economic and other opportunities, such protest was not clearly an effective way to do this. Washington thought that a better way was for blacks to advance economically, and consequently to give concrete demonstration – rather than to simply claim emptily – that they had the human capacity to reason intelligently, cooperate, restrain their appetites, and plan for the future. Since Washington urged blacks to advance economically, this suggests that we might have been mistaken when we speculated earlier that he was unaware that the claims implied in racial segregation were used to justify denying blacks economic opportunities. Perhaps Washington was aware of the function of these claims but was urging a way to offset and negate them that was different from and perhaps superior to Du Bois's. Indeed, he usually justified his case for black economic

[30] W. E. B. Du Bois, "Social Equality," p. 8.

advancement with the argument that such advancement would persuade whites to think well of blacks. "When a black man has the best farm to be found in the county," he once wrote, "every white man will respect him."[31]

It should also be noted that Du Bois's view, as I have tried to reconstruct it, does not show that the thesis that blacks tend to live in the opinion of whites is false. If that thesis is true, Du Bois's recommendations could be compromised, for his determination to gain the good opinions of whites could be driven by a feeling that he had to gain their approval in order to sustain his own self-respect, however much he might insist, that he was only trying to gain blacks' opportunities; and Washington's recommendations, on the other hand, could take on an unexpected depth and power. Indeed, Washington might have understood something that Du Bois did not understand, namely, that the way to make white affronts harmless to black self-respect – though certainly not less *offensive* to it – was for blacks to concentrate on becoming economically independent of whites. For if they succeeded, blacks would not gain their conception of themselves from whites' conception of them, and consequently would not gain a negative conception of themselves from whites' negative conception of them.

But I suggested earlier that protest as persuasion may be worse than merely possibly ineffective. I take up this possibility in the next section.

## II

According to Rousseau, serious fights were rare in the earlier stages of the state of nature when people had no pride. Sometimes, of course, two people might both want the same meal, and might seem ready to fight over it. But since neither resorted to blows "without first having compared the difficulty of prevailing with that of finding his sustenance elsewhere," they rarely fought, and when they did, their fights usually ended quickly and with little harm done. For, as

---

[31] Booker T. Washington, "Address delivered at Hampton Institute," in *African-American Social and Political Thought 1850–1920*, edited by Howard Brotz (New Brunswick: Transaction Publishers, 1992), p. 372.

Rousseau observed, "pride had no share" in such fights.[32] When the potential contenders were equally strong, aware of their equality, and consequently aware that the costs of fighting would be high, there would be even more reason to expect them not to fight.

Let us now complicate the case by introducing, one by one, pride and morality into Rousseau's state of nature, and by finally withdrawing the assumption that the contenders are equal. Suppose first that they are not only equally strong, but also that they are equally proud. In that case there will be considerable reason to expect them to fight, for, although each knows that fighting will bring severe losses, pride will allow neither of them to "back down." Suppose next that our equal contenders have both pride and a sense of justice. Rousseau implies that a sense of justice would further increase the likelihood that the contenders will fight, because it would give them another reason to fight. Here I disagree with Rousseau. A sense of justice will give the contenders another reason to fight, if they disagree on who ought to have the meal. But it also enables them to agree on who ought to have the meal, and if they do, the likelihood that they will fight, would fall dramatically, for although one of them would have to give up the meal, neither would think she was "backing down," given that persons with a sense of justice do not think that someone "backs down" if she gives up what is not hers because she thinks she ought to. Indeed, the one who gives up the meal because she thinks she ought to may even gratify her pride, for as even Hobbes allows, some people can feel considerable pride in *not* stooping to injustice.[33]

It will be objected that this argument assumes that the contenders will agree on who ought to have the meal, and there is no reason to believe that they will. But there is considerable reason to believe that they will. If most people have the capacity to be rational and to formulate and follow moral principles, then when they do not agree on a moral issue, one should suspect that they are not sufficiently motivated to find the correct solution to the issue, and consequently fail to present their own arguments carefully to their opponents, or

---

[32] Rousseau, "Discourse on Inequality," in Gourevitch, *Jean Jacques Rousseau*, p. 209.

[33] Thomas Hobbes, *Leviathan* (Oxford: Basil Blackwell, 1947), p. 92.

fail to attend carefully to their opponents' arguments.[34] But in the case at hand, the contenders will be powerfully motivated to find the correct solution to the issue that divides them. Each wants the meal and understands that the correct solution may assign it to him; and each understands that even if the correct solution does not assign him the meal it will at least enable them to avoid both the costs of fighting and the loss of face of backing down. Therefore each will present his own arguments carefully to his opponent, and each will attend carefully to his opponent's arguments.

It may be objected that the contenders will still be acting for prudential reasons, for they will still only be trying to save face, whereas my argument requires that they act for moral reasons. But if we can be motivated to act for moral reasons if we attend to such reasons carefully, we can be motivated to act for moral reasons, even if we attend to such reasons carefully because prudence and pride move us to do so. It may be objected that although people can be motivated to act for moral reasons if they attend to these moral reasons carefully, the contenders I have described do not attend carefully to the moral reasons for acting, but simply seize on these reasons as a face saving cover to avoid conflict. But this objection does not pay attention to my argument. I described the contenders as proud, not merely vain. Proud people do not only want to "save face" before others, but also to "save face" before themselves. That is, they do not only want *others* to think that they are not backing down; they want to convince *themselves* that they are not backing down. But they can only convince themselves that they are acting for moral reasons if they attend carefully to the reasons for acting morally. Consequently they will attend carefully to the reasons for acting morally. That is, neither will want to say, insincerely, that the other has a right to the meal – for this would injure her pride and self-respect, and, if her deception were uncovered, the respect the other had for her as well. And neither will want to be duped into saying the same thing; not only would this lose her the meal, which she wants, it would also diminish the other's respect for her sagacity

[34] Another possibility, of course, is that the issue is terribly complicated and they cannot find the solution. But although I allow, of course, that moral issues can be enormously complex, I must register my suspicion that complexity is often a ruse raised by one of the parties who wants to avoid finding a solution, and that this is most likely to happen when the contenders are not equal.

and alertness. But each will present the best arguments for her own case that she can, and each will very carefully study the other's argument. In that case, given that each has a sense of justice there is reason to expect that they will settle their dispute peacefully, act from a sense of justice, and lose neither pride or mutual respect.[35]

This argument suggests that contenders with pride and a sense of justice and an equal capacity (and willingness) to cause each other trouble have reason to be moved to honestly reflect on their options, and this may often, though certainly not inevitably, lead them to arrive at and act on correct moral conclusions. If it is sound, contenders with unequal capacity (or willingness) to cause each other trouble are much less likely to arrive at and act on correct moral conclusions – even if they each have a sense of justice. Consider, first, the stronger. Fearing few losses from fighting and robbing the weaker, prudence will give her little reason to attend carefully to the moral protests of the weaker, and since she does not contemplate backing down, her pride will give her little reason to reflect honestly on why she ought not to rob the weaker, at least if she wants what the weaker has. It may be objected that her pride in her own justice may move her to do this. But Hobbes was right that such pride was a rare trait, for usually it is subverted by self-interest.[36] That is, having decided to take advantage of the weaker, the stronger's pride in her own justice will usually only move her to construct sophistical arguments to justify herself.

Now consider the weaker. It may seem that he will have reason to appeal to morality, for he will think that it is the only thing he has on his side. But he does not have morality on his side. He may think so at first, and he might at that point try appealing to it, but as it becomes clear to him that stronger is not listening to him, and is apparently oblivious to morality or twists it in her interests, he will abandon morality and resort to any of a number of stratagems: He may try bluffing, exaggerating his own strength or desperateness; or he may advertise his wounds, and his victimhood, appealing to the stronger's pity; or, finally, retreating to what Berlin calls the "inner

[35] Of course, it is not guaranteed that they will do so, or that if they do that they will agree. Besides the possible complexity of the issue, they may be satisfied with a stand-off, or although the contenders each has a sense of justice they may believe in different principles of justice.

[36] Hobbes, *Leviathan*, p. 92.

citadel" he may play the Stoic, and put on a dignified air hoping to impress his oppressors- but still prudently give way on essentials.

This analysis does not merely suggest that the strong are likely to take advantage of the weak. It also suggests, more disturbingly, that the strong and the weak are not likely to engage in serious or honest discussion about the morality of their relationship. And we have not yet considered the consequences of Rousseau's thesis that if the weak "live in" the strong they tend to make the strong's conception of them their self-conception. In that case, since the strong are likely to have several different conceptions of the weak, and I have said nothing to suggest that the weak are entirely passive in their relationship with the strong, the weak's desire for necessities and their passion for the conveniences the strong control will move them to actively cultivate the conception the strong have of them that is most likely to persuade the strong to allow them access to the things they crave. But this conception is not likely to be one that stresses the weak's equal moral standing, though there is no reason to deny that the strong may in some veiled way conceive of the weak as their moral equals; this would be a non-starter because it would require the strong to give up more than they are prepared to give up. A more likely possibility is that if the strong conceive of the weak as pitiable, the weak will drift into encouraging that conception, for although pity may move the strong to succor and help those they conceive to be pitiable, it also insinuates their superiority, and consequently does not require them to give up very much. And there is a further consideration I have not yet mentioned. It would not be enough for the weak simply to cultivate the strong's conception of them as pitiable. This would win them few concessions if the strong were barely capable of pity, or cruel, hardened or insensitive. Consequently the weak must encourage the strong to think of themselves as sensitive, generous, benevolent, and in general, basically good, though their splendid enthusiasm for magnificent ends sometimes distracts them from attending to the mundane demands of the strictest justice. And since this is a somewhat flattering image the strong will encourage it and then begin to be fixated on the weak's conception of them. In other words the strong will begin to "live in the opinions" of the weak, just as the weak "live" in their opinions, and to share in the weak's disposition not to think honestly and critically about its own motives and behavior.

This analysis suggests that whites are not likely to attend carefully to black protest. The considerations already adduced will be compounded by the apparent complexity of the moral issues that divide whites and blacks.[37] Since the resolution of complex moral issues often requires gathering and marshalling large numbers of facts, and constructing elaborate arguments, and since being far more numerous, and usually better educated and funded, white experts will often be better at these tasks than black experts, they will often be able to outmaneuver their black opponents, gain the undivided attention of the public, persuade it that the black experts are manufacturing complaints, and encourage it to feel justified and complacent. I am not suggesting that white experts will do anything so crude as to deny, in this day and age, that blacks have natural or human rights. They denied this some years ago – and it may be noted, managed to hold their own, and create uncertainty in the public mind, for a considerable period – but today, everyone agrees that blacks have natural or human rights. The controversy now is what these rights involve or require, and how they can be compensated when they are violated, and since these issues can be very complex, there is considerable room for maneuvering, and creating distractions, and consequently for superior sophistication to be decisive, even against the truth.

The analysis also suggests that black protest is likely to compromised by blacks' desire to get at the necessities and conveniences whites control, to raise moral issues in way that tends to be indirect, veiled, twisted, dishonest, and even perverted. My suggestion that the weak are liable to present themselves as pitiable receives some confirmation in this particular case, by the long line of anti-protesters, from Booker T. Washington to Shelby Steele, who tell us that black protesters exaggerate their victimhood and are not interested in gaining respect for black rights, but in gaining crumbs from the white table. If they are correct – and I suspect they are not always mistaken, some protesters have done rather well for themselves – even if

[37] Though I still maintain that a considerable part of this complexity is a deliberately created ruse designed to confuse the issue and to avoid doing the just thing.

protester get what they crave, this is at the cost of encouraging whites to think of blacks as pitiable victims. The real worry here is not that the protester is a hypocrite, slyly pretending to be a pitiable victim, for the advantages this will bring him, knowing all the time that he is not. It is far more serious than that. If the weak get their conception of themselves from the conception the strong have of them – a conception they may also second and encourage – then the protester will think of himself as a pitiable victim. Now a person whose rights are violated is to that extent a victim, and can respect herself and be respected by others. But if she thinks herself as wholly a victim and encourages others to think of her that way, she denies and devalues her power to think, to plan and to set goals, that is, the powers that make her a person, and she is likely to be despised by those who witness her performance, and likely to despise herself. And we should add that the material advantages that such protest brings are likely to be distributed quite narrowly, mainly to the active protesters themselves. Their performance, if it is successful, will arouse the strong's pity, not her sense of justice – for though she can feel pity for one who is wholly a victim, she cannot respect him as someone to whom she owes justice. Consequently though protest may move her to pity and to reward the noisiest and most visible evidence of her wrongdoing, it will not move her to seriously reflect on it, or to undertake the broad-based reforms it calls for.

It may be objected that this assumes that the weak can form no independent conception of themselves, and that this is implausible even if the thesis of "life in others" is to some extent true. Or even if the weaker forms no independent conception of themselves, since the stronger have a variety of conceptions of the weak, the weak may cultivate the strong's image of themselves as victims, while simultaneously holding on to another conception the strong may have of them, perhaps that they are troublemakers. They would then be hypocrites, but at least they would not be servile, and in the circumstances perhaps the strategy would be justifiable. I wonder, however, whether it would be effective. Remember that the strong have armies of alert, highly intelligent and sophisticated experts to deal with the weak's complaints. If the "noble lies" of these complainants are to any degree detectable, these armies of experts will detect and expose them, disgrace the complainants and render them ineffective. Hasn't that happened often enough? And what if the lies are undetectable? Then one will have to wonder whether the liars will not begin to believe their lies. If it is hard for a person to maintain a conception of herself when no one seconds it, and the world at large affirms an opposite conception, how much harder this must be if she herself encourages and acts out the world's conception![38]

It may be objected that black history is full of sly black pretenders. I will be reminded of Sambo and Brier Rabbit. These figures are held to epitomize black slaves' ability to dupe the master with apparent servility, all the while being clear – behind their masks – of their own self-respect. For example, according to Orlando Patterson, Sambo was playing a "deadly serious game" in which his fawning and servility were a sham that won him concessions and enabled him to strike back at the system.[39] I am not persuaded. For how indeed did Sambo strike back at the system? Steal a few chickens? Break a few tools? I think the master saw through Sambo's tricks – they were transparent enough – and went along with them because it paid him to do so. Sambo broke tools and stole chickens to distract himself from his condition, and to maintain his sanity. I think the master understood this, and decided correctly that Sambo's petty infractions were a small price to pay to keep Sambo sane and distracted from his condition – and to keep himself master. And there was the bonus of the fun of duping Sambo when Sambo thought he was duping him. If this is correct, Sambo's attempts to strike back at the system helped to sustain it. It is possible, however, that Sambo was not even trying to strike back at the system. Patterson argues that Sambo did not cover up his thefts very carefully because he wanted his master to know he had stolen the chickens, and then to punish him and to thereby acknowledge his humanity. This is a poor argument because the masters punished their oxen and horses along with Sambo. My analysis offers a soberer and more accurate account of Sambo's motives. If Sambo wanted to get caught, it was more likely because he intuited that the master would be touched and amused by conceiving of him as a transparent trickster, in the way adults are touched and amused by a child's wiles they see through but pretend

[38] I have made some of these points in "Self-Respect and Protest," *Philosophy and Public Affairs* **6** (1976): 58–69.

[39] Orlando Patterson, "Toward a Future that has no Past-Reflections on the Fate of blacks in America," in *The Public Interest* **27** (1972): 25–62, at p. 42

not to see through to amuse themselves and the child, and Sambo encouraged the master to conceive of him in that way because he saw that it would win him favors.

Patterson may object that Sambo was trying to get his master to punish him in the way that he punished another person, not in the way he punished his oxen and horses. I concede that people punish persons differently from the way they punish animals; they punish animals simply to condition them to behave properly, but they punish persons for this reason and also because they believe that persons know the difference between right and wrong and sometimes do what they know to be wrong. I also concede that a slave might very well want to try to get his master to punish him in the way he punished a person. His object would not simply be to be acknowledged as a person by his master. Part of being a person is to be capable of getting things to happen that would not happen except for one's free and intentional intervention. Consequently to confirm his probably sagging sense of his own personhood the slave might not only want to be acknowledged as a person by his master, but might also want to get the master to do so himself, possibly by "tricking" the master into punishing him the way he punished a person. But it is preposterous to argue that Sambo was trying to "trick" the master into punishing him as a person. On the contrary, his petty chicken stealing and clumsy tool breaking were so much like a fox's petty chicken stealing, and an ox's clumsy tool breaking, that it seems more likely that he was trying to trick the master into punishing him like an animal. I do not deny that Sambo started off wanting to be treated like a person. But I am suggesting that his desire to win favors might have compromised this honorable motive and tricked him into acting as if he wanted to be treated like an animal.[40]

The desire to win favors may also compromise the weak's honorable motivation by tricking him into playing the part of the stoic. Consider, for example, Booker T. Washington. Washington did not engage in protest; indeed he was its greatest opponent. But in oppos-

---

[40] In the last few paragraphs I have added considerably to the doubts about Patterson's analysis of Sambo I expressed in "Self-Respect and Protest." For a different discussion of the Sambo issue and a thorough review of the literature, see Bill E. Lawson, "Oppression and Slavery," in *Between Slavery and Freedom*, by Howard McGary and Bill E. Lawson (Bloomington: Indiana University Press, 1992).

ing black protest, in advertising and emphasizing black stoicism and loyalty to whites, and in encouraging blacks to develop and display these qualities, he was himself cultivating a particular white conception of the Negro as loyal and stoic. Moreover, he was doing so for precisely the same reason he criticized the protesters for protesting – to impress powerful whites and persuade them to throw him some crumbs. It can be replied, on Washington's behalf, that the conception of blacks that his strategy encouraged whites and blacks to have was not quite as ignoble as the conception of blacks the protesters encouraged; certainly, it seems better to be a stoic than to be a whiner. But this is a short-sighted reply. The protester was not wrong to denounce the aggressor for wounding him. He was wrong only when to gain favors he acted as if he was nothing but a victim. Similarly, while loyalty and stoicism are normally good qualities, virtues even, it is foolish and servile to be loyal to those who betray and exploit you, and disloyal to justice to be stoical when stoicism gives even the appearance of acquiescing to injustice.

It may be objected that Washington wrote judicious letters to the newspapers lecturing whites on the dangers to themselves, of their injustice, and he was engaged in extensive behind-the-scenes activities designed to stop these injustices, although this was not widely known until several years after his death. But now a different difficulty arises. I mentioned earlier that the strong have armies of experts to detect and expose hypocritical protesters – those who do not really think of themselves as wholly victims. But, of course, these experts will not always expose the weak's duplicities, even when they detect these duplicities. They will allow these duplicities to stand when doing so serves their interest and the interest of the strong who hire them. This suggests that perhaps Washington's clandestine activity in support of black rights was not exposed because it served the interest of the strong to have the major black spokesman credibly urge blacks to be loyal and stoical. In other words it was a case of Sambo and the master all over again. Washington's masters saw through his tricks, but went along with them, pretending to be tricked, because doing so served their interests. Or perhaps, more ominously for Washington, he knew that his deceptions were detected and played the part of the ineffectual and transparent trickster who is unaware that he is detected because he knew his masters liked to think of blacks in that way, and rewarded blacks who were that way. Finally, and this would be the real tragedy, having cultivated the master's conception of him as such a trickster, Washington *became* such a trickster.

I think that it is such tortuous possibilities that have always moved the black nationalists to insist on self-help and to argue that blacks should become independent and powerful so that dealing with whites from a position of equal power they would not have to put on masks, or perhaps what is even more morally debilitating, have to wonder whether they were putting on masks, in order to try to get justice and respect from whites. But I cannot let the nationalists have the last word, and in the next section I sketch an argument that suggests that the nationalists' way may not be the only way.

## III

I begin by noting that Frederick Douglass called for black power as insistently as the nationalists. It was Douglass, after all, who wrote, "A man, without force, is without the essential dignity of humanity. Human nature is so constituted that it cannot honor a helpless man, although it can pity him; and even this it cannot do long, if signs of power do not arise."[41] When Douglass thus implied that black people had to acquire power in order to be honored and respected, he was certainly not endorsing the nationalists' argument that blacks should acquire the kind of power associated with economic and perhaps political independence, for he was the greatest opponent of the nationalists. What kind of power then was he implying that black people had to acquire in order to be honored and respected?

The best indication of the kind of power Douglass had in mind can be inferred from his account of the results of the fight between the slave woman Nellie Harris and the overseer Sevier. Sevier attempted to whip Harris, but Harris resisted heroically, and managed to give him a lot of trouble before he eventually overpowered her. Although Sevier then whipped Harris cruelly for having resisted him, more cruelly than if she had not resisted, both as an example to the other slaves and because she had angered him, he never again tried to

[41] Frederick Douglass, *My Bondage and My Freedom* (Urbana: University of Illinois Press, 1987), p. 151.

whip her. Douglass was deeply impressed by these events, and his reflections led him to coin the crude but effective aphorism, "He is whipped oftenest who is whipped easiest."[42]

The question for us is how it can be defended, and in particular, how to explain Sevier's restraint. One possibility is that he simply concluded that whipping Harris was too much trouble. This should alert us to a possible oversight in Rousseau's analysis. Rousseau implies that when the contenders for a meal in the state of nature have neither pride nor a sense of justice the weaker would invariably give way. This implication is false. Sometimes it could be the stronger who gives way, when for example, the weaker puts up a desperate fight, believing that the meal in contention is the only one he can get, and if the stronger calculates that the cost of subduing him is greater than the cost of her getting a meal somewhere else. Of course, the stronger could think it best to subdue the weaker even in these cases in order to establish her reputation as the stronger, and to avoid the costs of future fights; or she may suspect that the weaker is trying to appear more desperate than he really is, and calculate that it is worth her while to call his bluff.[43] Still, it is certainly possible that in some cases the stronger could calculate that on balance she could best serve her interests by letting the weaker have the meal. But this is less likely to happen after the contenders become proud. In that case the pride of the stronger would probably move her to subdue the weaker even at considerable cost to herself. But this should suggest that there is a flaw in the argument that Sevier failed to try to whip Harris because he calculated that the costs of trying to whip her were greater than the benefits; the violent pride of the typical slave overseer would never permit him to admit even to himself that he dared not whip a slave – especially a female slave! I submit that a better explanation of Sevier's restraint is that he concluded – no doubt grudgingly and reluctantly – that he ought not to whip Harris. It is a better explanation, for since one does not lose face by doing

[42] Douglass, *My Bondage and My Freedom,* pp. 61, 62.

[43] These complications may not be consistent with Rousseau's assumption that human beings are simple and naive in the period he is describing, but they are consistent with his condition that the human beings have no pride in that period, for a person who desires to have a good reputation because a good reputation is useful, need not be proud. I agree, of course, that a desire for the kind of reputation in question may lead to pride.

what one ought to do, it explains how Sevier's pride would allow him not to try to whip Harris.

This argument closely resembles the argument in Section II that if contenders for a meal in the state of nature are equal, self-interested, proud, and have a sense of justice, they will often be moved to discover, and to agree on, who ought to have the meal. But that argument seems to have assumed that the contenders were equal in destructive capacity, and Harris and Sevier were clearly unequal in that respect. Consequently critics may suspect that one or both of the arguments is unsound. But it was not essential to the earlier argument that the contenders were equal in destructive capacity; what was essential to that argument was that each of the contenders had enough destructive capacity, and displayed enough of a readiness to use it, to lead the other to conclude that the costs of fighting for the meal probably far outweighed the benefits. In that case, given that each would be tempted to back down, yet also reluctant to do so, for each was proud, each could be moved to try to discover and to agree on who ought to have the meal. For, as I argued, since each has a sense of justice, each would know that if he could give up the meal because he was convinced that he ought to, he would avoid both the costs of fighting for the meal and the loss of face of backing down.[44] Now, although the contenders' perception of their equal destructive capacity – and willingness to use it – could cause them to try to discover and agree on who ought to have the meal, a different perception could do as well.

Suppose that the contenders were unequal in destructive capacity, but that although the weaker could not cause the stronger as much trouble as the stronger could cause her, she was able and willing to cause him enough trouble to move him to wonder whether it might not be better if he backed down. In that case, since the stronger, being proud would be reluctant to back down, he could be moved to try to discover and to agree on who ought to have the meal for the same reasons that he tried to discover and to agree on who ought to have the meal when he faced a contender with the same destructive capacity as himself. That is, if he is proud, and therefore reluctant

[44] I am assuming, as I mentioned earlier, that people with a sense of justice do not feel that they have lost face if they give up what they believe another has a right to.

to give up the meal, he could begin to search for a way to give up the meal that was not backing down, and since one conspicuous way to do this would be to give up the meal because he believed that he (morally) ought to, he might begin to seriously consider the evidence in favor of the conclusion that he ought (morally) to give up the meal. I am suggesting that Harris accomplished something like this when she fought Sevier. If he tried to whip her and she resisted, she could not cause him as much trouble as he could cause her. Still, she was able and willing to cause him enough trouble to lead him to wonder whether he ought not to whip her; and in that case, given that he was proud and therefore reluctant not to whip her, for this could seem as if he were backing down, he would begin to search for a way to not whip her that was not backing down. But one conspicuous way to do this – if he had a sense of justice – would be to not whip her because he believed that he ought not (morally) to whip her. Consequently he might begin to carefully consider whether he ought not to whip her.[45]

It may be objected that this argument relies on the questionable assumption that Sevier had a sense of justice. I concede that my argument assumes that Sevier had a sense of justice, and I concede too that I could be wrong about this. But these concessions strengthen my overall analysis. The view that people like Sevier cannot have a sense of justice runs into the difficulty that such people often do things they could not do if they had no sense of justice, such as acting justly in certain contexts, and writing or speaking with great sensitivity and insight on questions of justice. Consider the case of Thomas Jefferson. Jefferson had his slaves whipped, and he was more guilty of the crimes of slavery than Sevier could ever be. But obviously he acted with justice on many occasions, and he could not, I think, have written the great lines of the Declaration of Independence if he had no sense of justice.

But even if Sevier had a sense of justice there was no guarantee that Harris's resistance would have the results that it did. For example, if Sevier was proud enough he might not have paused to wonder whether it would better for him not to whip Harris, even if the costs

[45] As I emphasized in the earlier argument in Section II, if the individual is proud, and not merely vain, he will be moved to discover what he really ought to do, not what he must do to save face before others.

of whipping her exceeded the benefits of doing so; but in that case he would not be moved to consider whether he ought not to whip her. But we must not read too much into his possibility. If Sevier was proud, he was also self-interested. Consequently if the costs of whipping Harris exceeded the benefits of doing so by a wide enough margin he would begin to wonder whether it was reasonable for him to indulge his pride and to whip her, and at that point, he would begin to look around for a way to save both his pride and the costs of trying to whip her. That is, as I have argued, he might begin to seriously consider that he ought not to whip her.

It may be objected that if the costs of whipping Harris exceeded the benefits of doing so by a margin that was so wide that Sevier began to think it unreasonable to indulge his pride and whip Harris, then at that point Sevier would simply decide on prudential grounds that he should not whip Harris; in particular, there is no reason to suppose that he would embark on a search for reasons why he ought (morally) not to whip Harris. But this objection misunderstands how pride works. Pride does not only move us to accept losses in order to confirm or establish our superiority; it also torments us when the costs of indulging it are so high that we yield to prudence. Thus, although a proud person may back down if the costs of acting as his pride dictates are high enough, he will not congratulate himself for being so reasonable! His pride will be wounded and it will blame himself for being a coward and for yielding to the crass calculation of costs and benefits. It will give him peace only if he has a sense of justice and can convince himself that he was not yielding to prudence but doing what he morally ought to do. If I am right about this, and if Sevier had a sense of justice, then I think my argument stands that his pride and the costs of whipping Harris, could well have moved him to embark on a search for reasons why he ought not to whip her.

But what if Sevier had no sense of justice, which I have conceded is possible? In that case he would be unable to avoid the predicament Harris put him in by convincing himself that he ought not to whip her, and he would either indulge his pride and whip her or kill her, or yield to prudence and, depending on his calculations, back down or whip her or kill her. Or even if he had a sense of justice, his pride – or perhaps his self-interest – could have persuaded him to whip her whatever the costs, or even to kill her. Douglass was well aware of the dangers and uncertainties in the course Harris pursued, for he followed his account of her fight with an account of an overseer who killed Denby, a rebellious slave, and claimed that he had to do so to maintain his authority over the slaves.[46] But Douglass was not arguing that the weak can always wring justice and respect from the strong, if they resist the strong heroically enough. Such an argument suggests that heroic resistance is compelling evidence of the weak's humanity, and that such evidence is bound to touch and persuade the strong of the weak's humanity. But the mature Douglass did not countenance such a view.[47] It suggests that before the fight Sevier might not have had sufficiently clear or compelling evidence of Harris's humanity. But if that were the case I cannot see why her resisting him could have persuaded him of her humanity, since to take her fighting him as evidence of her humanity he would have to believe things about her that would have been enough to persuade him of her humanity whether or not she resisted; after all squirrels fight when they are cornered, but I imagine that few are persuaded to infer the humanity of squirrels from this! My argument assumes that Sevier had ample evidence *all along* that Harris and all the slaves had rights, and that many if not all of them valued their rights; or at least that the evidence available to Sevier that Harris and the slaves had rights was no less than the evidence available to him that his wife and friends had rights. His problem, according to my argument, is that while he paid attention to the evidence that his wife and friends had rights, he did not pay attention to the evidence that Harris and the other slaves had rights. And what I want to suggest is not that Harris's heroic fight moved him to respect her because it gave him evidence that she had rights, but that it moved him to respect her because, in the way described, it moved him to pay attention to the evidence he had all along that she had rights. That is, Harris's fight

[46] Douglass, *My Bondage and My Freedom*, p. 79.

[47] In "Is it Right and Wise to Kill a Kidnapper?" Douglass argued that the public might be moved to seriously consider the slave's moral standing if he gave it evidence of his love of liberty by imperilling his life for his liberty. But Douglass quickly came to the conclusion that the public would not pay attention to this evidence of the slave's humanity unless its fear forced it to pay attention. I have developed this argument in "Fear and Shame as Forms of Moral Suasion in the Thought of Frederick Douglass," *Charles S. Peirce Society Proceedings* **21** (1995): 713–744. The present argument suggests another way that the strong can be forced to pay attention to the evidence of the humanity of the weak.

had its relatively happy result only because she was strong enough and willing enough to use her strength to lead Sevier, despite his pride, to wonder whether it would be better not to try to whip her. If she had been so physically weak that Sevier thought it child's play, or even good fun, to overpower her, he would probably have whipped her for the sport it gave him, however heroically she resisted – even if he had a sense of justice.

Now Harris did not fight Sevier and risk her life simply to avoid the pain of being whipped; a whipping was painful, but not that painful. Further, fighting Sevier was not a particularly good way for Harris to avoid being whipped; she almost certainly knew that Sevier would overpower her and whip her more cruelly for having resisted him. If all she wanted to do was to avoid the pain of being whipped her best bet would have been to avoid antagonizing Sevier at all costs, or if this could not be avoided, to beg forgiveness, or even to simply kill herself. And for the reasons I have given she certainly could not reasonably have fought Sevier anticipating the results that did occur. The most plausible explanation of her resistance was that she was moved by a profound sense that it was morally wrong and degrading to allow herself to be whipped without resisting. Now to have power in general is to have destructive capacity and to be willing to use it. Accordingly, given that Harris's willingness to use her destructive capacity against Sevier depended on her attachment to a moral principle, I think it is appropriate to call her power "moral power;" and supposing that her case was a model for the kind of power Douglass was recommending black people to acquire, I conclude that the kind of power he was calling black people to acquire was moral power.

It may be pointed out that the weak may resist the strong though not because of an attachment to a moral principle, and consequently that they may have a power that is not moral power. I agree, of course, but my point was that Douglass was calling on black people to acquire specifically moral power. And there is also reason to believe that moral power is more likely to have the moral effects on the stronger that I described than power acquired in some other way. Suppose, for example, that at some point the weak become so miserable that instinct takes over and they resist desperately like animals. I suspect that in such cases the stronger are likely to take their behavior as proof that they are somewhat less than fully human, and consequently would not embark on the moral reflections I described. The weak do not have to give the strong evidence of their humanity to persuade the strong of their humanity (for the strong have plenty of such evidence already), but they are unlikely to persuade the strong of their humanity if they behave in a way that confirms the strong's prejudice that they are less than human.[48] This suggests that there is no reason to deny that the weak's heroic resistance may function as compelling evidence that helps to persuade the strong to acknowledge the weak's humanity – at least if the strong are given some reason to pay attention to that evidence, and to interpret it correctly.

If I am right about this the nationalists' way is not the only way that blacks can get justice and respect from whites. Their way requires that blacks acquire the same conventional power as whites, but if Douglass is right, blacks may have the moral power to get justice and respect from whites even if they do not match whites in conventional power. Someone may wonder why Douglass thought it necessary to argue that moral power could help bring the stronger to their moral senses. Why was he not satisfied to show simply that it could win the weak their rights? Surely that would be enough to justify it, whether or not it also moved the strong to believe that the weak had rights. But the uncertain peace that is based on a mere balance of power is not enough; peace can be secure only if people genuinely respect each other's moral standing. Consequently, I think Douglass's purpose in arguing that moral power could have moral effects was to remind us that a readiness to use force may have a justification that is higher and more compelling than the argument that it can help establish a balance of power.

The risks associated with the exercises of moral power suggest that it may lessen the dangers of persuasive protest, if it is used in conjunction with such protest. A protester who risks his life to defend his rights is not likely to have compromised his moral position by a desire to win favors! On the other hand, the risks associated

48 The best indication that Douglass took this view is in his account of his own fight against Edward Covey the "slave breaker." Douglass did not fight like an animal. On the contrary he emphasized the restrained way that he fought. See Douglass, *My Bondage and My Freedom*, p. 151. I have analysed Douglass's account of that fight in "The Fight with Covey," in Lewis R. Gordon, ed., *Existence in Black* (New York: Routledge, 1997), pp. 273–290.

with the exercise of moral power also suggest that it will be used only in extreme circumstances; for example, Douglass did not urge exercises of moral power after the abolition of slavery. It may be useful therefore to note briefly that Martin Luther King's conception of civil disobedience may be a version of Douglass's view adapted to less extreme circumstances. Here it may be useful to distinguish King's conception of civil disobedience from that of John Rawls. Rawls suggests that the public may be moved to respect the sincerity and conscientiousness of civil disobedients when it sees them accepting punishment for breaking a law they consider unjust, and that as a result it might be moved to consider their complaints seriously. In particular, he does not think that the civil disobedients have to threaten the public's interests to get its attention. On the contrary he argues that this would be a distraction.[49] King, however, argued that the civil disobedients had to cause or threaten the violators with enough trouble to persuade them to listen to what the civil disobedients were saying.[50] King's views are therefore close to Douglass's on how the weak can move powerful wrongdoers to serious moral reflection.[51]

## IV

The considerations advanced in this essay help explain why the kind of legal victory that Plessy sought for blacks often does not produce all the results its advocates hope for. Since the public is usually not compelled to seriously consider the legal and moral arguments for the victory, it is rarely converted, and after a short period of confusion and indecision it quickly regroups and finds a way to circumvent the victory or even to use it to whites' advantage. But we should not

---

[49] John Rawls, "Definition and Justification of Civil Disobedience," in Hugo Adam Bedau, editor, *Civil Disobedience in Focus* (New York: Routledge, 1991), pp. 106, 107.

[50] Martin Luther King, "Letter from Birmingham City Jail," in Bedau, *Civil Disobedience in Focus,* p. 70.

[51] Part of the difference between Rawls and Douglass here is that Rawls thought of civil disobedience as suitable for a "nearly just" society, whereas Douglass was proposing strategies for a society that still allowed slavery. But at one time, in particular, in "Is it Right and Wise to Kill a Kidnapper?" Douglass endorsed a strategy strikingly like Rawls's account of civil disobedience. See note [47].

conclude with observers like Bell that racism is permanent. There has been solid progress (though far from enough), although that progress has never been due to the persuasive power of protest alone. It has been due to such protest plus the growing economic power of the black community and its occasional readiness to use its moral power in the way Douglass and King recommended.

But the analysis behind these conclusions may strike some critics as too pessimistic. They may complain that the strong do not always exploit the weak, or at least do not often do so with a clear conscience. I agree, of course. The strong's capacity to exploit the weak with a clear conscience will often be moderated by sympathy and other sentiments, and the strong will ignore the weak when the weak have nothing the strong want. However, when the strong see the weak as also strange and foreign, my argument that they will rob and exploit them, and think well of themselves for doing so, is amply confirmed by the history of the meetings of strong and weak peoples. The more interesting objection is that my account is too optimistic. Those who raise this objection believe that power corrupts and that the strong tend to lose all sense of justice, or to be so self-deceived and incapable of clear thinking that the weak can never move them to think carefully and cogently in the way I have suggested. I have no reason to deny that the corruption they describe is possible. Indeed, some of my arguments indicate how it can develop. But it is rarer than they seem to think. Despite Plato, the strong are often mentally and morally healthy, even when they are guilty of great injustices. This will be a disappointment to those who believe that injustice never pays and that cosmic justice punishes wrongdoers. But the weak deceive themselves, and lapse into pessimism, or make their struggle for justice more difficult than it need be, if they take comfort in that belief.[52]

Department of Philosophy
The University of North Carolina at Chapel Hill
CB 3125 Caldwell Hall,
Chapel Hill, NC 27799–3125 U.S.A.

[52] I wish to thank Thomas Hill and Jan Boxill for helpful discussion. Special thanks to Gerald Postema for forcing me to give the argument in Section III the clarity that it has.